Pinch-Dash-Done

A Gateway to Flavorful Recipes

Credits

_____

Photos by
Ken Jones Photography

Logo and Graphic Designs by
St. Walls Collection

Editing By
McWriting Services
Sharon Jenkins

www.pinch-dash-done.com

Library of Congress Number 2020917171

ISBN # 97817355463-1-5

Thank you for helping provide *food for better lives*. More than 1.1 million people in the 18 southeast Texas counties served by Houston Food Bank are considered "food insecure," meaning they lack consistent access to enough nutritious food to fuel a healthy life. In order to address this issue, the Houston Food Bank distributes food and other essentials to those in need through a network of 1,500 community partners including pantries, soup kitchens, social service providers, and schools. In addition, Houston Food Bank also provides programs and services aimed at helping families achieve long-term stability including nutrition education, job training, health management, and assistance in securing state-funded assistance.

Foreword by
Dr. Ruth J. Simmons
President of Prairie View A&M University

Having grown up around master cooks of traditional southern black fare, I was not aware of the genre of cookbooks that represented the modern evolution of regional and cultural cuisine. That is, not until I met and worked with Rima Drell Reck, a professor at the University of New Orleans.

After taking up an assistant professorship in French at the University of New Orleans, I soon learned that Rima was working on a volume on New Orleans cuisine. I was more than mildly interested in the project because I had just moved to New Orleans and felt pressure to learn how to cook Cajun and Creole staples such as red beans and rice, gumbos, and etouffees. I was delighted to see the finished product: a cookbook that went far beyond simply detailing the ingredients and cooking of classic dishes; her book revealed the historical and cultural perspective, bringing a broader understanding of the ways in which we should appreciate distinctive cuisines as manifestations of the role of food in how we understand the history and culture of the peoples who created them. From then on, I was hooked on reading cookbooks for such revelations.

With *Pinch-Dash-Done,* Vernita Harris and Beatrice Moore have collaborated to bring us a book that offers similar benefits. To scan the list of recipes they offer is to understand the evolution of modern cuisine throughout the diaspora. From the days of minimal access to variety, their recipes reveal the ways in which communities today have evolved to an array of healthier ingredients and styles that remain rooted in traditional fare. For example, homemade ice cream, a longtime staple of family and church gatherings, shows up in eight different versions to delight the modern palette.

In survival-guide mode, their recipes remain simple and healthy. This approach aligns well with the impetus for the volume: to earn funds for donations to the Houston Food Bank and Prairie View A&M University. Both institutions are active in providing healthy food, with Prairie View having established its own food bank for students who are food insecure.

We live today in an era of increased interest in food. Recent generations seem more interested than ever in how food is grown and prepared, its nutritional value, and its sustainability. Those who are able to try the recipes in this volume will no doubt experience, like every cookbook lover, a foray into this new era where a pinch here, a dash there, produces a new world of food preparation uniquely suitable for these times.

RUTH J. SIMMONS

ABOUT THE AUTHOR

Vernita B. Harris,

better known as *"The Reluctant Cook"* of this cooking duo, has years of cooking and global dining experiences. Although she has enjoyed taking cooking classes in Italy and sat at numerous chef's tables, she never considered herself a cook. Vernita often mused, "If I had to cook, I could and knowing that was always enough." In Spring 2020 everything changed, not only was she forced to cook but families across the globe found themselves in the same predicament. Vernita quickly dusted away all the cobwebs of cooking and went back to Grandma's kitchen, her mother's baking, college and church fish and chicken dinners sales, family and friend's potluck gatherings, and home economic classes from high school. However, it was the Italian grilling that impressed her the most and gave her a familiar and comfortable place to revive her dormant cooking skills. It would have been easy for her to say "I can't do that". But instead, she took all her past culinary experiences and said "Why not?" As a result of her personal resolve and need to survive, she revived what had been planted in her long ago, tested recipes, and finally documented them in this collection of recipes.

A proud native Houstonian, Vernita is a serial entrepreneur with several businesses under her belt and is currently operating developments domestically and internationally. She holds two degrees from Prairie View A&M University- a BA in Marketing (79) and an MBA in Management (81). She left corporate America in 2006 and never looked back. Her strength lies within business strategic planning. Her motto is "Cultivating solutions is what I do best". Over the years, Vernita has garnered several business awards and accolades for exemplary leadership. Marketing was always been her strength. As a matter of fact, she still has textbooks from her first college course,

Marketing 101! Two of the most important lessons she learned was that the basics don't change, but trends do and preparation is key.

She is from a large blue-collar family with 7 siblings. Some of her fondest memories of growing up are food centered-there was always food being prepared on the stovetop, oven or her Dad's custom bar-b-que pit. As one of the three girls, she watched her Mother create magic with a modest budget and few ingredients. She was a real cook! Everyone knew, not to be slow getting to the dinner table. Vernita doesn't recall all that her mother did in the kitchen, but she did notice how her mother altered recipes to create her own more improved versions. Proving that the apple doesn't fall too far from the tree, Vernita has also taken that same approach to creative cooking-adjusting spices, sugars, milk... to transcend basic recipes and enhance flavors that are exciting to the palate.

Vernita considers herself a "foodie". Her favorite three cities in the world are Houston, Texas, Florence, Italy and Freeport, Bahamas. She lived in Italy for 2 years and currently lives in Freeport, Bahamas. Each city has their own unique culinary creations that resonate in her cooking preference. The most evident is her choice of spices. Vernita is drawn to grilling since she is a reluctant cook and this is an easy option for favorable and fast meals.

This book is a gift of Vernita's love of food and celebration of creating memories while dining with family and friends. Gateway will provide a variety of options that are designed to broaden your sense of taste and meal selections. Vernita has published 6 books and this is her first effort in writing a cookbook. She is proud to add her independent contributions to this collective and humbly share them with you and your family.

Happy Cooking from "The Reluctant Cook!"

ABOUT THE AUTHOR

Beatrice (Bea) Moore

is a native of San Antonio, Texas, but her roots run deep into the landscape of the river bottoms of the Guadalupe River where, she spent much of her time as a child with her grandparents Jesus and Malvenor Garcia. It was those times spent on an active farm that gave her a love of gardening and cooking with farm-fresh ingredients and cooking from scratch— often with no recipe— and learning the tools and rules of the kitchen.

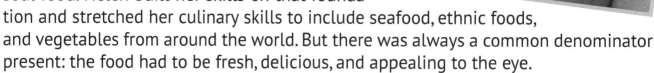

Her grandmother was an excellent cook who knew how to take a little and make a lot from it. Bea's other cooking inspiration was her mother, Helen. She worked as a head cook in a number of hotels and eventually began her own catering business. Malvenor and Helen had areas of expertise in different types of food. Malvenor mastered the art of the casserole and traditional southern soul food. Helen built her skills on that foundation and stretched her culinary skills to include seafood, ethnic foods, and vegetables from around the world. But there was always a common denominator present: the food had to be fresh, delicious, and appealing to the eye.

Bea paid attention, incorporated all she had learned, and began to experiment with different flavors, spices and recipes to develop her own unique cooking signature that honors her diverse heritage. Cooking is a passion and an act of love for Bea. She approaches cooking in an organic way, following her sense of taste and combining unusual herbs and seasonings to create complex layers of taste. One of her fondest memories of time spent with her mother was eating out and analyzing the spices used in the meal. They would then challenge themselves to not just reconstruct it, but to improve it! She loves to surprise the taste buds by introducing less familiar ingredients to salads and desserts such as dried lavender and rose! Hosting dinner parties is one of the ways Bea has shared her gift of cooking. She is also an avid gardener who believes that every home should have a sustainable garden, complete with a compost bin—a definite nod to her agrarian upbringing.

Bea is a proud graduate of Prairie View A&M University and holds a BS in Mathematics. She went on to obtain a MA in Curriculum & Instruction and has spent the bulk of her career in Mathematics Education as a secondary mathematics teacher, district supervisor, mathematics coach, and independent consultant. She has seamlessly integrated her Texas Lifetime Secondary Teacher Certifications in the areas of Mathematics, Spanish, and Journalism into her work with various programs to support improved instruction with a focus on equity and providing support for underrepresented student populations. She has had the honor of working with numerous state and national projects and grants. Through her work in these areas, she has traveled extensively, working in 47 states, Canada, Bermuda, and the Caribbean. Her exposure to these different geographical regions also enlarged her appreciation for unfamiliar foods and cooking methods, which have been incorporated into the recipes she shares in *Pinch-Dash-Done*.

During the COVID-19 pandemic of 2020, Bea found herself with more time to experiment with recipes and began sharing ideas online with friends; this was the birthing point of *Pinch-Dash-Done*. The publication of this cookbook is her first venture in the world of cooking, but she is not new to authorship. She has published two fiction novels, a faith-based and a non-fiction publication, a multitude of professional articles, and mathematics textbooks for Algebra I and II and grades 6-8.

Bea welcomes you to *Pinch-Dash-Done*. Feel free to modify and experiment with the recipes and create your own signature dishes that are as unique and as special as you.

Bon Appetit from the "Passionate Cook!"

Dedications

Bea

To my beloved grandmother, Malvenor Garcia, who instilled in me a love for the garden. To my wonderful mother, Helen, a consummate chef whose love of life and cooking were contagious. To my dearest Aunt Verlene, who reminded me that there were short-cuts in the kitchen. To my darling children—Macy, DJ, and Curtis—who stretched my skills and imagination with weeknight dinners, I thank you. I love you. I look forward to the day when we may all be gathered at the table together again. Until then...

Vernita

To my sweet grandmother, Ellen Jones, who always had tasty food on the stove for anyone that walked through the door, and to my parents, David and Willie Harris, Jr., who kept eight kids fed on the smallest of budgets by utilizing the stovetop, oven, refrigerator, and bar-b-cue pit (the original food processors!) to ensure that the family had healthy and delicious meals at all times. Inclusion in the process was much more than just licking the spoon—you provided a rock-solid foundation, and for that, I dedicate this book to the three of you. I love and miss you all!

Pinch-Dash-Done
A Gateway to Flavorful Recipes

Introduction

Pinch-Dash-Done, LLC is a new company introducing its first edition *A Gateway to Flavorful Recipes* to audiences of all ages to help with mindful and uncomplicated menus. The inspiration behind this concept came during the shutdown of 2020. There was an outpouring from our social media family and friends for positive stories and ideas. Vernita Harris and Beatrice (Bea) Moore, two college friends, decided to share recipes and menus suggestions in their posts. Our family and friends looked forward to easy recipes and creative ways to spice up meals during this period. A revival of cooking is one of the positive residual effects of the shut-in/lockdown and stay-safe initiative. People need food to survive and we were providing simple ideas to enhance mealtimes. Your palate will travel via Tex-Mex, Southern, Italian and Caribbean influences throughout the book.

Our Audience

In this edition, *A Gateway to Flavorful Recipes* is geared to support the diverse needs of individuals and families who desire quick, easy ideas to mix up the palate, novice cooks who may doubt their culinary skills, seasoned cooks who need to spice up their repertoire of recipes, and health-conscious cooks craving substance and flavor. This easy-to-follow cookbook will be great for all ages, from elementary school to seasoned citizens!

Philanthropic Goals

Bea and Vernita are both community advocates. After watching the negative impact on the food supplies during the spring of 2020, they felt compelled to find a way to serve the community and address food insecurity on a long- and short-term basis. Subsequently, they decided to invest their stimulus checks and personal investments into the creation of Pinch-Dash-Done, LLC. Their desire for this cookbook is to serve as a vehicle to provide funding to the following institutions that directly impact food insecurity.

Founded in 1982, Houston Food Bank is America's largest food bank in distribution, leading hunger relief in 18 southeast Texas counties. Donations from sales of *Pinch-Dash-Done A Gateway to Flavorful Recipes* will help with tackling the short-term issue of food shortages. For more information on Houston Food Bank, please go to www.houstonfoodbank.org.

Both authors are proud alumnae of Prairie View A&M University, where they met during the spring semester of 1976. Established in 1876, Prairie View A&M University is the second-oldest public university in the state of Texas. Because of its agricultural and mechanical focus, Bea and Vernita plan to establish a scholarship endowment to assist students that are economically challenged in safeguarding a quality education. The newly-created scholarships will support students majoring in Agribusiness and will promote domestic and international food systems and supply chains. These donations will contribute to the long-term goal of overcoming food insecurity. For more information on Prairie View Agricultural & Mechanical University, please go to www.pvamu.edu.

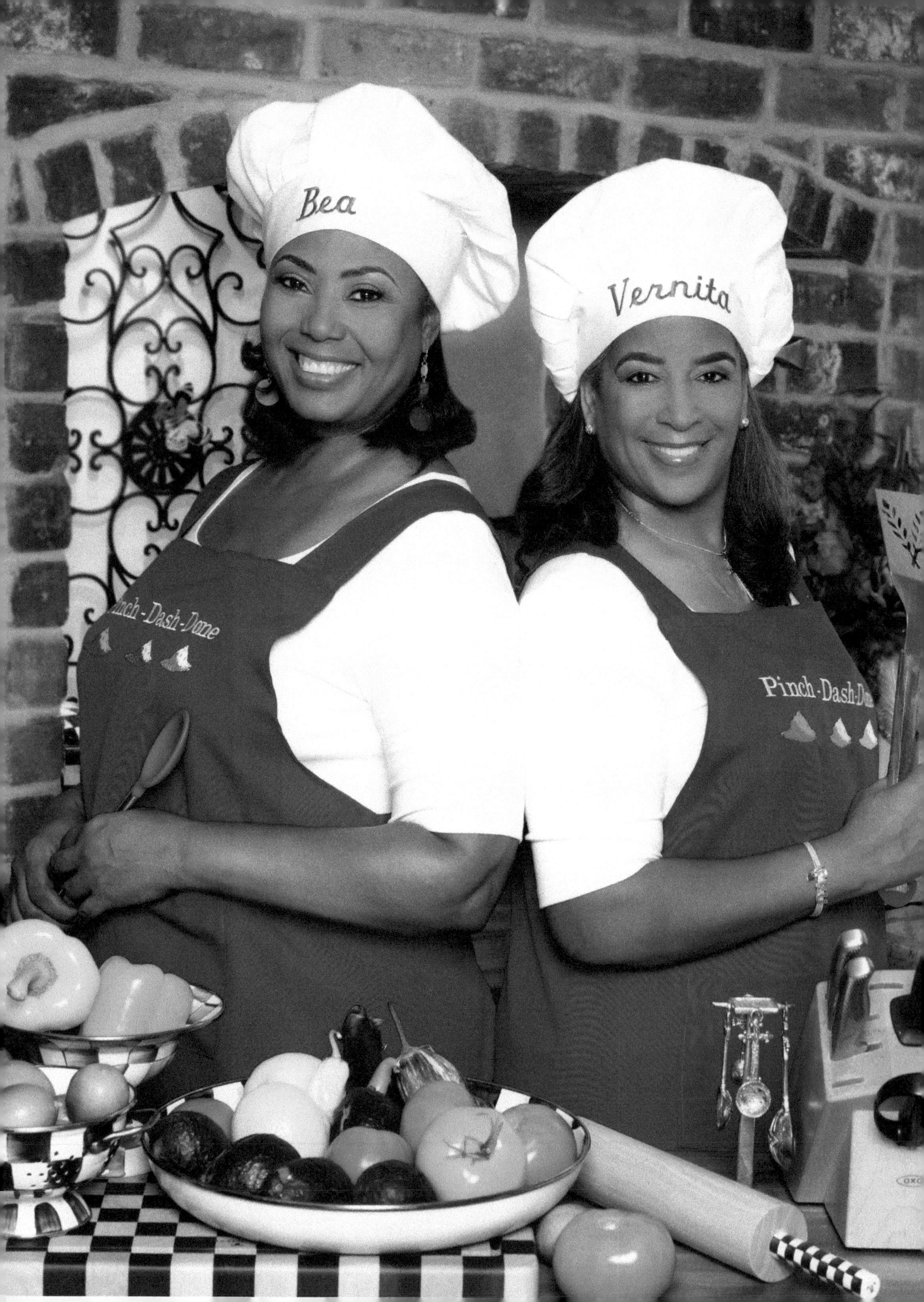

Bea
Vernita
Pinch-Dash-Done

Table of Contents

DESSERTS

BREADS AND BUTTERS

DRESSINGS, SAUCES, PESTO, AND DIPS

SALADS

ENTREES

SOUPS & STEWS

LITE BITES

SIDES & VEGAN

BREAKFAST AND BRUNCH

INDEX

DISCLAIMER

THANK YOU

Kitchen Must Haves

Must Haves
Beatrice
Lemons
Olive Oil
Cumin
Chili Powder
Shallots
Sweet Potatoes
Jalapeños
Heavy Cream / Half-and-Half
Chicken Broth
Avocados

Must Haves
Vernita
Dill – weed / seed
Cilantro
Garlic
Basil
Wheat Pasta
Bell Peppers – tri color
Coconut Milk
Zatarain's Crab Boil
Carrots
Ginger

Must Haves
Staples
Condiments – mayonnaise, ketchup, mustard
Vanilla Extract
Cooking Oil – vegetable
Flour
Sugar – brown / white
Salt – sea / fine / Kosher
Pepper – red / black / white
Lettuce
Tomatoes
Bread – buns / wheat / white / rolls

HERBS

From Your Farm to Your Table: Eight Easy & Essential Herbs

The Benefits of Growing Your Own Herb Garden

In researching, testing, and creating our recipes for *Pinch-Dash-Done A Gateway to Flavorful Recipes*, we realized that we have eight essential herbs that are used throughout our recipe collection: basil, chives, cilantro, dill, mint, oregano, parsley, and rosemary. Not only are they essential, they are easy to grow indoors or out and do not require much maintenance. Although many dried herbs are readily available, there is nothing like a pinch or dash of fresh herbs to elevate the taste! Additionally, adding fresh herbs to your diet is a great way to boost your meal's vitamin value—and if you grow your own, it is a money saver!

One of the goals of *Pinch-Dash-Done A Gateway to Flavorful Recipes* is to revive fellowship around the dining table among generations. We also realize that herb gardening is a valuable educational experience for all ages, promotes sustainable gardening on a small scale, and is also a great way to bond as a family as you explore, test, and create memories through food experiences.

Growing your own herbs means that you'll always have more than you can possibly use, leaving you plenty of extras to share with friends, family, and neighbors as you share recipes and cooking tips. Additionally, having an herb garden allows you to have quality control of the herbs as well as peace of mind in knowing that your family is eating not only fresh, but also pesticide-free herbs.

As you contemplate the creation of your herb garden, remember that you have the option to grow from seed or purchase seedlings and starter plants from local nurseries. Good nurseries have knowledgeable staff who can educate you about soil conditioning and alert you to any issues that may arise regarding pests. But not all bugs are bad! Growing your herbs outdoors is beneficial to sustaining populations of bees and other helpful insects (and another good reason not to use pesticides).

Remember, herbs are easy to grow, don't take up much space, may be indoors or outdoors, and are adaptable to most climates.

BASIL

With dozens of types to choose from, basil satisfies almost any palate. It is well-known as the main ingredient in pesto, as you will find in our upcoming chapter on pesto. However, do not restrict the use of basil—be adventurous! Although the "Genovese" or sweet basil variety is most-commonly used, there are other varieties to explore and they each have their own distinctive palate signature. Some basils impart anise, lemon, mint, cinnamon, or clove flavors to foods. For example, lemon basil is very reminiscent of lemon zest. This aromatic basil is a great addition to fish, especially a salad served with cold salmon. My personal favorite is purple basil, which has distinctive purple foliage, a slightly spicy, clove-like flavor, and attractive blooms which attract bees and butterflies to the herb garden.

Basil is a great addition to your herb garden and does best when grown in full sun. It cannot tolerate freezing temperatures but it will drop seeds and you will be greeted by new plants every year. Basil also does well in container gardens or indoors in a sunny window, but use a pot large enough to allow the basil to expand and yield a generous harvest. The more you harvest basil, the more it will produce.

CHIVES

Chives are not just for topping baked potatoes! They are one of the most well-known herbs and are extremely easy to grow—but often one of the least used. Chives may impart either an onion or garlic flavor, thus making them a great substitute for onion or garlic in both raw dishes such as salads and cooked dishes. They help you "feast with your eyes" since they retain their vibrant green color even when cooked. They also make a great garnish.

Chives do require full sun and will benefit from rich, moist soils. If you notice yellow stems, don't fret. These are simply the chive leaves that have finished their growing cycle. All you need to do is simply

remove them. If you plant your chives in the garden, it is best to split them up every two to three years in early spring by digging up the entire clump and dividing it into two or three clumps, which you can then plant separately or share with friends! Chives will also grow very well indoors on a windowsill. In fact, they will grow almost anywhere as long as they don't get too dry.

CILANTRO

Cilantro's flavor and odor are quite pungent. It tastes and smells a bit like a more-citrusy version of parsley and is sometimes mistaken for it. Interestingly, a few people may find that cilantro also tastes slightly *soapy*—those individuals actually have an uncommon genetic variation in their taste buds that allows them to pick up on the soapy flavor of a naturally-occurring chemical called *Aldehyde* in the leaves, which most of us cannot taste. Cilantro makes a good complement to spicy foods and is commonly used in Asian, Mexican, and Indian cuisines. The leaves are also sometimes referred to as "Chinese Parsley." Additionally, the dried seeds of the cilantro plant are *coriander seeds* (which have a warm and spicy flavor completely different from the plant leaf). Many dressings, soups, dips, sides, and meat dishes incorporate cilantro.

Cilantro plants will *bolt*—meaning go to seed—as the days get longer and the temperatures rise (typically above 75°F), so make sure they are in a spot with full sun, or partial shade if you live in a particularly hot climate. Cilantro cannot tolerate cold temperatures. If there is any danger of frost, protect cilantro plants that are grown in the garden with a covering. When harvesting, pick leaves one by one or cut a third of the way down with kitchen or pruning shears, so that the remaining plant can continue to produce cilantro.

DILL

Dill pickles. This is what comes to mind most frequently when the herb dill is mentioned. But do not underestimate the power of this herb—it is much more versatile than you might think. You may use the seeds, flowers, and ferny foliage to season foods, or in other words, the entire plant is edible. Dill is a delicious compliment to fish and is often used to infuse vinegars. It is also used in a variety of dips, soups, and salads.

Dill is a standout star in the garden with its lovely golden-yellow, umbrella-shaped blooms. It needs full sun. The root system is shallow and strong winds can sometimes topple the dill plants with their delicate, spindly structure, so you may wish to choose your garden location with this in mind. Dill cannot tolerate cold temperatures below 40 degrees.

The general rule is to harvest the leaves as needed, the flowers as they open, and the seeds just as they ripen. If some seeds are allowed to ripen on the plant, the plant will self-seed and volunteer seedlings will appear in the garden the next year—much like the basil plant. But gardeners beware—dill attracts beneficial insects (bees love it) but also draws predatory insects such as wasps to the garden.

MINT

Spearmint, peppermint, grapefruit, strawberry, lemon, and chocolate mint are just a few of the many mint varieties that are available. Mint is a traditional favorite with lamb and used in many Mediterranean cuisines. Mint is also wonderful paired with chocolate desserts, and the leaves add a terrific pop of flavor to tea, water, salads, and more!

Mint is super easy to grow and does best in partial shade but can handle full sun if kept moist. It is also an aggressive grower—if you plant it in an outdoor garden, it is best that it is planted in a confined space such as between the house and driveway so that it will not encroach other beds. Because of the spreading pattern of growth, it makes a good ground cover as well. If you prefer, you can grow it in a container to prevent it overtaking the garden.

OREGANO

There are many varieties of oregano—Greek, Italian, Cuban, Mexican—just to name a few. Fresh oregano is a great companion to pasta, pesto, sauces, meats, dressings, and salads. It also dries beautifully and can be enjoyed year-round. (Note that the flavor of oregano intensifies as it dries so you would typically use much less of it in dried form than fresh.)

This aromatic, nutritious herb prefers low humidity and can be grown in containers or in the garden. If grown in containers, beware that the roots suffer if there is too much moisture, so a well-drained pot and loose soil is a must, along with good air circulation. If planted in the ground, it makes a great ground cover but it does spread if not groomed often. It may be harvested at any time. Cut back the foliage several times throughout the year to encourage new growth. Harvest by cutting the stem and removing the leaves.

PARSLEY

There are two types of parsley: curly and flat-leaf. Both are easy to grow but have different uses. Curly parsley has a very subtle, mild flavor and is commonly used for garnishing plates, often along with a fruit slice. The curly leaves require more effort to wash than the flat-leaved type. You may chop it finely and use curly parsley as called for in recipes, although in general, the curly variety is more closely associated with decoration. Flat-leaf parsley has a more robust flavor and is typically preferred in cooking, but you can use whichever you like best—when substituting one for the other, taste to determine the flavor and adjust as desired. Think, too, about the texture that would work best in your dish. Parsley is an immensely popular herb that adds a fragrant, fresh nuance of flavor to a wide variety of dishes. And don't discard the stems either, which have a stronger flavor than the leaves, as they can be used in a bouquet garni and added to homemade stock or a pot of beans.

Parsley is a low-maintenance plant that needs full sun to partial shade, regular water, and occasional feeding. It grows well in containers. You must harvest regularly to promote growth.

ROSEMARY

Rosemary is very versatile. It is a pungent, strong, finely-needled herb that is peppery, sage-like, slightly bitter, and woody/balsamic in flavor. It is used as a seasoning in a variety of dishes, such as soups, casseroles, salads, and stews. It also enhances the flavor of poultry, lamb, pork, steaks, and oily fish. Rosemary pairs well with grains, mushrooms, onions, peas, potatoes, and spinach. It is a must have! It may be grown in the garden or in a container. Plus, it is an evergreen, so you will have the benefits of fresh rosemary year-round.

Rosemary prefers full sun. And, as with most plants and herbs, proper watering is essential to successful growth. The best way to determine if a rosemary plant grown in a container needs water is to insert your finger into the soil. If the top one-to-two inches of soil feels dry, it is time to water. Growing rosemary in pots placed near entry doors is not only attractive, but the oils of the plant are released if touched or watered and the aroma fills the air—it is a fresh, piney, welcoming scent.

DRINKS

White Sangria

2 cups pinot grigio
2 cups tequila
2 cups ruby red grapefruit juice
1 cup simple syrup
1 cup fresh lime juice
2 cups ice
2 cups club soda
Slices of lime, grapefruit, and lemons (for garnish)
Mint sprigs (for garnish)

DIRECTIONS

Add the first five ingredients to a large pitcher or drink dispenser (except for the club soda, ice, and garnish). Add ice and slowly pour in the club soda; stir gently. Pour into individual glasses and serve with additional fruit and mint garnish.

Pomegranate Margaritas

1/4 cup sugar
1/4 cup hot water
1-1/2 cups pomegranate juice
3/4 cup tequila
1/2 cup fresh-squeezed lime juice
1/4 cup orange liqueur
Ice
Lime and lemon slices (optional, for garnish)

DIRECTIONS

Stir together sugar and hot water until sugar is completely dissolved. Stir in pomegranate juice, tequila, lime juice and orange liqueur. Pour desired amount into a shaker and add ice. Pour into chilled cocktail glass. Repeat until all mixture is used. Garnish with lime and lemon slices if desired.

Notes

Rosemary's Limon-Ade

8 tablespoons limoncello
1 bottle of sparkling white wine
4 rosemary sprigs (for garnish)
4 lemon slices (for garnish)

DIRECTIONS

Pour 2 tablespoons limoncello into
each of 4 champagne glasses. Top
with sparkling white wine. Garnish
with a sprig of rosemary and slice
of lemon.

Basil Orange Juice

1/4 cup basil leaves
1 quart (4 cups) fresh orange juice

DIRECTIONS

Muddle the basil leaves in the bottom of pitcher. Add orange juice and stir.

Notes

Coconutty Lemonade Slush

    1 pint (2 cups) lemon sorbet, frozen
    3/4 cup unsweetened coconut milk
    1/4 cup water
    1/4 cup frozen raspberries

DIRECTIONS

Combine all ingredients in a blender and puree until smooth. Pour into glasses and serve immediately.

Ginger Root Lemonade

    1 medium-sized ginger root (peeled and cut into chunks)
    1/4 cup light brown sugar or honey
    1 large lemon or lime (sliced and seeded)
    1/2 gallon (8 cups) water
    2 cinnamon sticks and/or whole cloves

DIRECTIONS

Add ginger root to the 1/2 gallon of water and bring to a boil. Cover the pot, reduce heat to medium, and let mixture simmer. Remove from the heat and let cool for 30-40 minutes. When mixture is lukewarm, stir in the sugar, add some of the lemon or lime slices (but save a few slices for garnishing later), and the cinnamon sticks and/or cloves. Cover and continue to steep until completely cooled. Once cooled, place in refrigerator until ready to serve. Pour into serving pitcher, garnish with more lemon slices and ginger and serve.

Notes

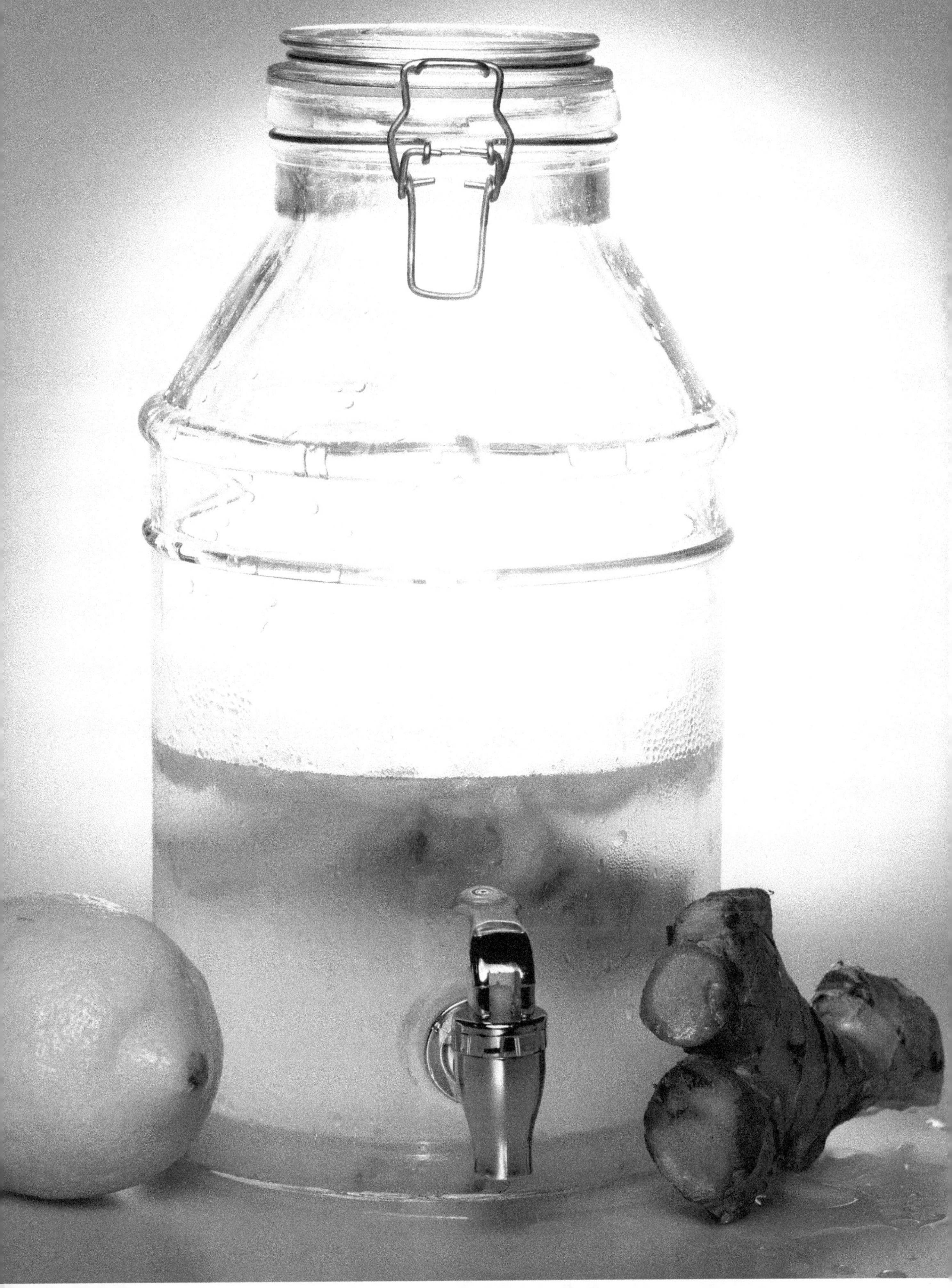

Peach Passionfruit Punch

2 scoops Lipton's Peach Iced Tea Mix
1 cup passionfruit juice or syrup
1 orange (sliced and seeded)
1 lemon (sliced and seeded)
1liter sparkling water or ginger ale
    (sugar free optional), chilled
1 cup rum (optional)

DIRECTIONS

Place orange and lemon slices in a container and freeze ahead of preparation. Mix all the remaining ingredients in a 2-liter pitcher. Caution—foam will rise while adding the sparkling water or ginger ale, so add that very slowly. Add frozen lemon and orange slices and serve.

Shanghai Tea

3 lemongrass stalks (cut into 3-inch pieces)
6 cups water
6 mint tea bags
1/4 cup honey

DIRECTIONS

Lightly smash the lemongrass stalks and add to water in a large pot. Bring water to a boil, then take off the heat. Pour into a heat-proof container and add mint tea bags and honey. Let cool and steep overnight in the refrigerator. Strain over ice and serve.

Notes

Pineapple Twist

16 oz. pineapple juice
8 oz. bottled ginger juice
2 tablespoons lemon juice
1 tablespoon honey
About 12 fresh mint leaves
Additional mint sprigs (for garnish)

DIRECTIONS

Mix all liquids in a tall pitcher; stir vigorously to incorporate the honey. Add mint leaves and muddle. Strain to remove the muddled leaves. Pour over ice into individual glasses and garnish with a spring of mint.

Banana-Mango Smoothie

1 banana (sliced)
1/2 of a fresh, ripe mango (sliced or cut into chunks)
1/4 cup carrots (grated)
1/2 cup coconut milk
1/2 cup kale leaves (chopped)

DIRECTIONS

Place banana, mango and carrots in a container and freeze. Put the frozen fruit into blender (which serves as the ice since there is none in the actual recipe). Add the remaining ingredients and blend until smooth consistency. Serve immediately.

Notes

Luscious Avocado Smoothie

1 large avocado (peeled and chunked)

1 teaspoon lemon juice
1 tablespoon honey
1/2 teaspoon ginger (dried, powdered)
1 cup fresh, ripe mango
1 cup ice
1 tablespoon soaked chia seeds (optional)

DIRECTIONS

Blend avocado with lemon juice, honey, ginger, mango and ice. (You may adjust the amounts of lemon juice, honey, and ginger to suite your taste.) Stir in soaked chia seeds for an omega-3 boost.

Notes

Green Pineapple Smoothie

2 cups frozen pineapple chunks
2 cups peeled cucumber chunks
1 cup celery chunks
2 tablespoons fresh sweet basil
2 teaspoons lime juice
1 cup water
Pinch of salt
1/2 cup ice
Celery stalks or basil springs (for garnish)

DIRECTIONS

Place all ingredients into blender and puree until smooth. Garnish with celery stalks or basil springs.

Notes

Watermelon Sunrise

1/2 of a small watermelon, seeded and cut into cubes
1/4 cup fresh-squeezed lemon juice
8-10 fresh mint leaves
3 tablespoons honey
Mint springs (for garnish)
Sliced lemon (for garnish)

DIRECTIONS

Place all ingredients in blender (except for garnishes) and puree. Pour over ice and garnish with mint sprig and lemon slice.

Notes

DESSERTS

Peppermint Ice Cream

3/4 cup whole milk
1/2 cup granulated sugar
Pinch of salt
1-1/2 cups heavy cream
1 tablespoon peppermint extract
4 peppermint twist candies
Peppermint sticks
       (optional, for garnish)

DIRECTIONS

Mix all ingredients together except for the peppermint twist candies and garnish. Stir well, making sure the sugar is fully dissolved. Let cool in refrigerator for 2 hours. Add chilled mixture to your ice cream maker and follow manufacturer's directions. Meanwhile, in a plastic bag, smash the peppermint twist candies into tiny pieces. With 2 to 3 minutes left to go with the ice cream, add the smashed bits of peppermint twist candy. Let cure in freezer for 1 hour and serve with peppermint sticks as a garnish (optional).

Notes

Lavender Ice Cream

2/3 cup half-and-half
1/3 cup fresh lavender flowers or
      2 tablespoons dried lavender flowers
2/3 cup sugar
4 egg yolks (lightly beaten)
2/3 cup heavy whipping cream

DIRECTIONS

In a small saucepan, heat the half-and-half to 175°F and remove from the heat; add lavender. Cover and steep for 20 minutes. Strain, discarding the lavender. Return to the heat; stir in sugar until dissolved. Whisk a small amount of the hot mixture into the egg yolks. Return all to the pan, whisking constantly. Cook and stir over low heat until mixture reaches at least 160°F and coats the back of a metal spoon. Remove from the heat. Cool quickly by placing pan in a bowl of ice water; stir for 2 minutes. Stir in whipping cream. Press waxed paper onto the surface of the custard mixture (which prevents a skin from forming). Refrigerate for several hours or overnight. Fill cylinder of ice cream freezer; freeze according to the manufacturer's directions. When ice cream is frozen, transfer to a freezer container; freeze for 2-4 hours before serving.

Amaretto Ice Cream

3/4 cup coconut milk
1/2 cup granulated sugar
Pinch of salt
1-1/2 cups half-and-half (fat-free works well also)
1 tablespoon rum extract
1/2 cup Amaretto liqueur (contains alcohol)

DIRECTIONS

Mix all ingredients, stirring well until sugar is fully dissolved. Refrigerate at least 2 hours. Add mixture to your ice cream maker and follow manufacturer's directions. Let cure in freezer for 1 hour before serving.

Oh-So-Easy Honey Vanilla Ice Cream

2 quarts half-and-half
1-1/2 cups honey
2 tablespoons vanilla extract
Rock salt
Ice

DIRECTIONS

Stir together all ingredients and pour into freezer container of traditional electric ice cream maker. Freeze according to the manufacturer's directions (using the ice and rock salt). Let stand 1 hour before serving.

Coconut Vanilla Ice Cream

(2) 14-oz. cans of full-fat coconut milk
   or 3-1/2 cups of coconut milk or heavy cream
1/3 to1/2 cup of honey or sweetener of choice
   (adjusted to taste)
2 tablespoons vanilla extract

DIRECTIONS

Combine the ingredients, whisking to get the honey to combine with the coconut milk, or simply blend in a blender. Make into ice cream according to the directions on your ice cream maker. You can serve as a soft serve right away or let cure in freezer for 1 hour and serve.

Notes

Coconut Brownie Ice Cream Sliders

Cooking spray
1 cup all-purpose flour, spooned and leveled
1/2 cup unsweetened cocoa powder
1/4 teaspoon kosher salt
1 cup (2 sticks) unsalted butter (cut up)
8 oz. bittersweet chocolate (chopped)
1-1/2 cups white granulated sugar
4 large eggs (lightly beaten)
3 pints (6 cups) coconut ice cream (softened)
Shredded coconut, for coating

DIRECTIONS

Preheat the oven to 325°F. Lightly grease an 18x13-inch rectangular rimmed baking sheet with cooking spray; line with parchment paper, leaving a 3-inch overhang on the two long sides. Whisk together flour, cocoa, and salt in a bowl. Microwave butter and chocolate in 30-second increments, stirring in between, until melted. Whisk in sugar. Whisk in eggs, just until combined. Fold in flour mixture, just until combined. Transfer batter to prepared pan. Bake until a wooden pick inserted in the center comes out with moist crumbs attached, 9 to 11 minutes. Cool completely in pan.

While still in the pan, slice brownie in half crosswise (so you have two halves). Freeze, in pan, until firm, at least 30 minutes. Remove one brownie half, and invert second brownie half in pan. Scoop coconut ice cream onto inverted brownie, and top with remaining brownie half (top side up) to create one giant sandwich; gently press together. Freeze, in pan, until firm, 1 hour or up to 2 days. Cut evenly into 12, single-servings sandwiches. Coat edges with the shredded coconut. (You may toast the coconut first, if desired.)

Notes

Passionfruit Ice Cream

 3/4 cups coconut milk
 1/2 cup granulated sugar
 Pinch kosher salt
 1-1/2 cups half-and-half (fat-free)
 1/2 cup passionfruit syrup or juice

DIRECTIONS

Mix all ingredients, stirring well, making sure sugar is completely dissolved. Place in refrigerator for 2 hours. Add refrigerated mixture to ice cream maker and follow manufacturer's directions. Serve soft or let cure in freezer for 1 hour and serve.

Notes

Limoncello Ice Cream

 3/4 cup whole milk
 1/2 cup granulated sugar
 Pinch kosher salt
 1-1/2 cups half-and-half (fat-free)
 1/2 cup Limoncello (contains alcohol)
 1 teaspoon vanilla exact
 1 tablespoon lemon zest
 Juice of 1 lemon

DIRECTIONS

Mix all ingredients in a large bowl, making sure sugar is completely dissolved. Let chill in refrigerator for at least 2 hours. Add mixture to ice cream maker and follow manufacturer instructions. Serve soft or let cure in freezer for 1 hour and serve.

Notes

Red, White, and Blue Drunken Sundae

- 1/2 cup black currant, or any red or blue
    fruit-flavored liqueur
- 1/2 cup fresh raspberries or strawberries
- 1/2 cup fresh blackberries
- 1/4 cup packed light brown sugar
- 3 cups vanilla ice cream
- Whipped cream
- Mint (for garnish)
- *4-6 Stroopwafel cookies*

DIRECTIONS

In a small saucepan, combine liqueur, raspberries, blackberries, and brown sugar. Bring to a boil and reduce heat. Simmer and stir occasionally until mixture begins to thicken, about 15 minutes. Remove from heat and allow to cool. If sauce becomes too thick, add about 1 tablespoon water (a little at a time) and stir until desired consistency. Scoop 1/3 to 1/2 cup of ice cream into each serving bowl and insert a Stroopwafel cookie into the side. Top with the cooled sauce mixture. Add a dollop of whip cream and spring of mint to finish the sundae.

Makes 4-6 servings.

Broken waffle cone or graham cracker cookie may be substituted for Stroopwafel cookie.

Amaretto Fruit Cake

1 seedless watermelon
1 8-oz cream cheese brick (softened)
8 oz. whipped cream (fat free)
1/4 cup brown sugar
6-7 strawberries (or fruit of choice)
1/4 cup of Amaretto liqueur (alcohol)

DIRECTIONS

Cut watermelon into 2- or 3-inch slices, shaped to resemble cake layers. Trim away and discard the rind. In a medium bowl, blend cream cheese and brown sugar. Fold in the whipped cream, and slowly add amaretto. Frost the watermelon sliced with this cream cheese mixture just like a tiered cake. Garnish top with sliced strawberries. Chill until ready to serve.

Note: The cream cheese mixture can also be used as a fruit dip.

Notes

Toasted Pound Cake with Sweet-and-Savory Strawberries and Basil

1 dozen fresh strawberries (rinsed, stems removed, and sliced)
4 tablespoons granulated sugar
2 tablespoons balsamic vinegar
8 fresh sweet basil leaves (thinly sliced)
4 slices of pound cake
1 tablespoon butter (melted)
1 cup Greek yogurt
2 tablespoons honey

DIRECTIONS

Gently mix strawberries, sugar, and balsamic vinegar together in a large bowl. Let sit at room temperature for about 20 minutes to allow the strawberries to release their juices but not get mushy. Mix yogurt and honey in a separate, small bowl. Just before serving, add the basil to the strawberries and gently toss. Heat griddle pan to medium heat. Take each slice of pound cake and lightly brush each side with melted butter and lightly brown each side on the griddle. Top off each slice of toasted pound cake with the strawberry mixture and garnish with a dollop of honey yogurt.

Bananas Foster Bread Pudding

For the sauce:

1/2 cup butter
1-1/3 cup dark brown sugar
7 tablespoons rum
3 tablespoons vanilla extract
1 teaspoon ground cinnamon
2 cups white chocolate morsels
5 cups heavy whipping cream
6 bananas (peeled and sliced)

DIRECTIONS

In a large deep skillet on medium heat, melt butter and add all ingredients except bananas. Once the mixture is bubbly add bananas and stir, blending the bananas into the mixture. Keep warm. Reserve about half of the sauce for plating.

For the bread pudding:

6-8-large croissants
8 slices brioche bread
1 cup golden raisins
1 cup chopped dried apricots
1 cup white sugar
Nuts of choice (for garnish)

DIRECTIONS

Prepare an 11x17 pan by rubbing it with butter. Preheat the oven to 300°F. Tear apart croissants and brioche into large bite sized pieces and place in large bowl with raisins and apricots. Pour half the sauce over the mixture. If mixture is too dry, add heavy cream in small amounts until desired consistency is achieved. After mixing the sauce with the croissants and brioche, place into the prepared 11x17 pan. Bake about 45 minutes. Allow to cool. When plating, top with the reserved sauce and any nuts of your choice.

Notes

Strawberry Sweets Bread

3/4 cup granulated sugar
1/2 cup milk
1/2 cup vegetable oil
1 large egg
1 teaspoon vanilla or almond extract
2 cups all-purpose flour
2 teaspoons baking powder
1/4 teaspoon salt
2 cups strawberries (diced)
2 tablespoons all-purpose flour

Glaze:

2 cups powdered sugar
2 tablespoons melted butter
1/3 cup strawberries (finely diced)
1/2 teaspoon vanilla or almond extract
1-2 tablespoons heavy cream or milk (optional)

DIRECTIONS

Preheat the oven to 350°F. In a medium bowl, stir together the sugar, milk, oil, egg, and vanilla (or almond) extract. In a separate bowl, combine the flour, baking powder and salt. Add the dry ingredients to the wet ingredients and stir until just combined. In a small bowl, toss together the strawberries and the 2 tablespoons of flour to coat the strawberries. Fold the floured strawberries gently into the batter. (The flour keeps the pieces of strawberry from sinking to the bottom.) Pour the bread batter into a greased 9x5-inch bread pan. Bake for 50-55 minutes. A toothpick inserted in the center of the bread should come out clean. Allow the bread to cool for 10 minutes, then remove the bread from the pan to a wire rack to cool completely.

To make the glaze, combine the powdered sugar, melted butter, diced strawberries, extract, and milk in a small bowl. Mix until it is smooth. Once the bread is cool, spread the glaze on top of the bread. Slice and serve.

Notes

Kentucky Derby Pecan Pie

1/2 package of refrigerated pie dough
Cooking spray
3/4 cup pecan halves
1/4 cup pecans (chopped)
1/2 cup pure maple syrup
1/2 cup dark corn syrup
3 tablespoons brown sugar
2 tablespoons butter (melted)
2 tablespoons bourbon
1 tablespoon pecan liqueur
1 teaspoon vanilla extract
1/4 teaspoon salt
2 large eggs (beaten)
2 large egg whites (lightly beaten)

DIRECTIONS

Preheat the oven to 350°F. Roll dough into a 12-inch circle and place into a spray-coated, 9-inch pie pan. Drape excess crust over the edge of the pan and pinch the edges to form fluted edges. Chill in freezer for 15 minutes. Combine the pecans and remaining ingredients into a bowl, stirring to combine. Pour filling into prepared crust. Bake for 35-40 minutes or until center is set. Shield the edges from burning with foil if necessary. Cool for at least 15 minutes before serving.

Notes

Caramel-Pecan Frosted Sheet Cake

For cake:

1 package white cake mix
1 cup buttermilk
1/3 cup butter
4 egg whites
1/4 teaspoon almond extract
Caramel Pecan Frosting

DIRECTIONS

Preheat the oven to 350°F. Beat together first five ingredients on low speed with electric mixer until well mixed. Pour batter into greased 15x10-inch pan. Bake for 15-20 minutes. Cool for 2 hours.

Caramel Pecan Frosting:

1 cup chopped pecans
1/2 cup butter
1 cup light brown sugar (packed)
1/4 cup buttermilk
2 cups powdered sugar
1/2 teaspoon vanilla extract
1/4 teaspoon almond extract

DIRECTIONS

Place chopped pecans in a single layer in a shallow pan and bake for 6 minutes at 350°F. Bring butter and brown sugar to boil in a 3-1/2 quart saucepan over medium heat, whisking constantly until well blended. Remove from heat and add buttermilk. Return to heat and bring to a boil. Immediately pour into bowl and mix. Gradually add powdered sugar, almond extract, and vanilla extract, beating at medium speed with electric mixer until smooth; stir in pecans and use immediately to frost the cake.

Notes

Lemon-n-Lavender Yogurt Loaf

1-1/2 cups all-purpose flour
2 teaspoons baking powder
1/2 teaspoon salt
1 cup plain yogurt
1-1/3 cups sugar
3 extra large eggs
2 teaspoons lemon zest
1/2 teaspoon pure vanilla extract
1/2 cup vegetable oil
1/3 cup freshly squeezed lemon juice

Glaze:

1 cup confectioners' sugar
2 tablespoons freshly-squeezed lemon juice
1tablespoon lavender extract

DIRECTIONS

Preheat the oven to 350°F. Grease an 8-1/2 x 4-1/4 x 2-1/2-inch loaf pan. Line the bottom with parchment paper. Grease and flour the pan. Sift together the flour, baking powder, and salt into a small bowl. In a separate large bowl, whisk together the yogurt, 1 cup sugar, the eggs, lemon zest, and vanilla. Slowly whisk the dry ingredients into the wet ingredients. With a rubber spatula, fold the vegetable oil into the batter, making sure it's all incorporated. Pour the batter into the prepared pan and bake for about 50 minutes, or until a cake tester placed in the center of the loaf comes out clean. Meanwhile, cook the 1/3 cup lemon juice and remaining 1/3 cup sugar in a small pan until the sugar dissolves and the mixture is clear. Set aside. When the cake is done, allow it to cool in the pan for 10 minutes. Carefully place on a baking rack over a sheet pan. While the cake is still warm, pour the lemon-sugar mixture over the cake and allow it to soak in. Cool. For the glaze, combine the confectioners' sugar, lavender extract, and lemon juice and pour over the cake.

Notes

Egg Wash

1 egg
2 tablespoons water

DIRECTIONS

Prepare egg wash by combining the egg and water and stirring well. Apply lightly to top pie crust with brush for an attractive, glossy finish. (Works great on breads and rolls as well, and is used in the following Peach Cobbler Minis recipe also.)

Peach Cobbler Minis

(1) 29 oz. can of sliced peaches in
    heavy syrup
1 stick butter
Juice of 1 lime
1/4 cup sugar
1 teaspoon vanilla
1 teaspoon cinnamon
1/2 teaspoon nutmeg
1/2 tablespoon vanilla
2 tablespoons pecan praline liqueur
1 box refrigerated pie crust rolls

DIRECTIONS

Preheat the oven to 375°F. In 2-quart pot, heat peaches with the juice from the can with lime juice, butter, nutmeg, cinnamon, vanilla and sugar. Bring to boil and reduce and simmer for 15 minutes. Add liqueur.

Unroll dough and press into greased 10- to 12-ounce oven-safe ramekins. Tear away any dough that overhangs the side. Place in oven for 5 minutes. Fill ramekins with peach mixture and cover the top of the mini cobbler with remaining dough. Prepare egg wash by combining the egg and water and stirring well. Vent and brush top of crust with egg wash and sprinkle with cinnamon, nutmeg and sugar. Place ramekins on oven safe cookie sheet. Bake until crust is golden brown.

Blue and Blackberry Cobbler

1-quart (4 cups) blueberries
1-pint (2 cups) blackberries
1 stick butter
1 tablespoon vanilla extract
1/4 cup raspberry liqueur
1/4 cup sugar
Juice of 1 lime
1 box refrigerated pie crust rolls

DIRECTIONS

Preheat the oven to 375°F. In 2-quart pot, heat berries with lime juice, butter, vanilla, and sugar. Bring to boil and reduce and simmer for 15 minutes. Add liqueur. Unroll dough and press into greased 8-inch pie plate. Tear away any dough that overhangs the side. Place in oven for 5 minutes. Fill heated pie crust with berry mixture and cover the top of cobbler with remaining dough. Vent and brush top of crust with egg wash and sprinkle with sugar. Bake until crust is golden brown.

Notes

Creamy Lemon Fruit Dip

1/2 cup heavy whipping cream
2 tablespoons granulated sugar
1 tablespoon lemon extract
1/4 tablespoon lemon zest

DIRECTIONS

In a large bowl, mix whipping cream and sugar. Blend in the extract and zest. Continue to blend for 3-5 minutes until creamy, but do not over-blend. Chill in refrigerator for at least 1 hour. Serve with fruit kabobs.

Notes

Fruit Kabobs

Watermelon (cut into cubes)
Cantaloupe (cut into cubes)
Apples slices
Whole Strawberries

DIRECTIONS

Place fruit onto fruit skewers, alternating fruits as desired. Serve with Creamy Lemon Fruit Dip or your dip of choice (optional).

Notes

Ziair's Oatmeal Ginger Pecan Cookies

2 sticks (1 cup) salted butter,
    softened to room temperature
1/2 cup granulated sugar
3/4 cup light brown sugar
2 eggs
2 teaspoons vanilla extract
1 cup all-purpose flour
1 teaspoon baking soda
1 teaspoon ginger or cinnamon (optional)
2-1/2 cups uncooked oats
1 cup chopped pecans (or walnuts)

DIRECTIONS

Mix softened butter and sugars together with mixer or by hand until smooth. Add eggs and vanilla to batter; mix well. Add the dry ingredients in slowly (but not the oats or pecans). Mix thoroughly and slowly add in oats. Add pecans in slowly. Chill in refrigerator the day before or an hour before cooking. Preheat oven to 350°F. Place mounds of cookie dough (about 2 tablespoons each) on greased or nonstick cookie sheet. Garnish the top with a few nuts of choice. Place on bottom rack of oven for 5 minutes. Raise the cookie sheet to the top shelf of the oven and bake for another 5-6 minutes, or until golden brown. Remove and let cool on the sheet for 4-5 minutes before removing.

Notes

Frozen Strawberry Yogurt

4 cups strawberries (frozen)
3 tablespoons honey
½ cup Greek yogurt
1 tablespoon fresh lime juice
½ teaspoon vanilla extract
Mint leaves
Fresh strawberries

DIRECTIONS

Place all ingredients except mint and fresh strawberries in blender and blend until smooth. Place in freezer for 10-15 minutes before serving. Garnish with fresh mint and fresh strawberries.

Notes

BREADS AND BUTTERS

Hollering Jalapeño Cornbread

1 package Jiffy Cornbread Mix
1 egg
1/3 cup milk
1/2 cup sharp Cheddar cheese (shredded)
1/2 can (4 oz.) whole kernel sweet corn
1/4 cup sweet onions (finely chopped)
3 tablespoons fresh jalapeños (chopped seeds removed)
3 tablespoons butter

DIRECTIONS

Preheat the oven to 400°F. Place 3 tablespoons butter in 9-inch baking pan and place in oven until butter is browning. Mix all ingredients together and spoon into the baking pan. Top the cornbread with a few jalapeño slices and a light sprinkle of cheese. Bake 15-20 minutes, or until golden brown. (The top will "spring back" when you touch it when done.)

Heavenly Cornbread

1 package Jiffy Cornbread Mix
3/4 cup half-and-half
3 tablespoons butter

DIRECTIONS

Preheat the oven to 400°F degrees. Place 3 tablespoons butter in 9-inch baking pan and place in oven until butter is browning. Mix all ingredients together and spoon into the baking pan. Bake 20 minutes, or until golden brown. (The top will "spring back" when you touch it when done.)

Notes

Herbed Cornbread

1 package cornbread mix
1/4 cup half-and-half
1/2 cup buttermilk
2 teaspoons herb seasoning
    (Mediterranean or Tuscan)
1/2 teaspoon dried sage
3 tablespoons butter

DIRECTIONS

Preheat the oven to 400°F. Place 3 table-spoons butter in 9-inch baking pan and place in oven until butter is browning. Mix all ingredients together and pour into the heated baking pan. Bake 20 minutes, or until golden brown. (The top will "spring back" when you touch it when done.)

Notes

Pistachio, Pecan, and Dates Whole Wheat Loaf

2 tablespoons vegetable oil
1-1/2 cups hot water
1 cup pitted dates (chopped)
1 large egg
1 teaspoon pure vanilla extract
1 cup unbleached all-purpose flour
1 cup whole-wheat flour
1 teaspoon baking soda
3/4 teaspoon kosher salt
3/4 cup pecans (toasted and chopped)
1/4 cup pistachios (toasted and chopped)
1-3/4 cup packed light brown sugar
2 tablespoons glazed pecans (crushed)

DIRECTIONS

Preheat the oven to 350°F. Lightly coat a 9-by-5-inch loaf pan with oil or non-stick baking spray. In a medium bowl, pour hot water over dates and let stand until slightly softened, about 5 minutes. Whisk in oil, egg, and vanilla. In another bowl, stir together flours, baking soda, salt, pecans, and brown sugar. Fold egg mixture into flour mixture until just combined. Pour batter into prepared pan and smooth the top with a spatula. Lightly sprinkle crushed nuts over the top. Bake, rotating pan halfway through, until a tester inserted in center of loaf comes out clean, about 1 hour. Let cool in pan on a wire rack, 20 minutes, then turn out bread and let cool completely.

Notes

Banana Nut Muffins

1 stick (1/2 cup) salted butter (softened)
3/4 cup light brown sugar
1 teaspoon vanilla
2 eggs
1 cup flour
1 cup uncooked oatmeal
1/2 cup coconut milk
1 teaspoon baking soda
3 ripe bananas (mashed)
1 cup pecan or walnuts (chopped)

DIRECTIONS

Grease muffin pan or place paper cupcake holders in muffin pan. Preheat the oven to 375°F. In mixing bowl, blend butter and sugar with wooden spoon together until smooth. Add vanilla and eggs, blend well. Pour in coconut milk. Continue to blend. Stir in flour and baking soda. Add oatmeal until well blended. Stir in bananas, leaving some lumps. Add nuts, saving a few for topping. Spoon batter into muffin tins. Sprinkle a few nuts on top. Bake 25-30 minutes. Test with toothpick to check for doneness. Let cool for 10 minutes then switch over to cooling rack. Muffins will freeze well in sealed plastic bag.

Spinach & Parm Warm Crostini

1 (10 oz.) package frozen spinach (thawed)
1 (8 oz.) package cream cheese (softened to room temperature)
1 cup freshly grated Parmesan cheese
1/4 cup mayonnaise
1 large garlic clove (minced)
1/4 teaspoon black pepper
1/2 (16 oz.) French bread loaf, cut diagonally into 1/2-inch slices
1/3 cup pine nuts

DIRECTIONS

Preheat the oven to 350°F. Drain spinach, removing all excess water. In a large bowl, stir together spinach, cream cheese, parmesan cheese, mayonnaise, garlic, and pepper. Top each slice of bread with the mixture, and sprinkle with pine nuts, place on baking sheet. Bake for about 10 minutes or until pine nuts are toasted. Serve immediately.

Garlic Butter

2 sticks (1 cup) real butter,
    softened to room temperature
1 teaspoon salt
Pepper to taste
1 teaspoon Italian seasoning
2 tablespoons fresh garlic (finely minced)

DIRECTIONS

Combine all ingredients in mixing bowl and whisk together. (Using an electric blender will incorporate more air and make it fluffy if you desire.) Use right away or refrigerate. Store in tight container and use within a week.

Notes

Honey Butter

2 sticks (1 cup) salted real butter (softened to room temperature)
2/3 cup honey
1/2 cup powdered sugar

DIRECTIONS

Place butter in a medium mixing bowl and beat for 2-3 minutes until light and fluffy. Add powdered sugar and beat for another minute. Add honey and continue beating until smooth and fluffy. Serve at room temperature for best results. Store in refrigerator in tightly sealed container. For best results, use within 3-4 weeks.

Herbed Butter

1/2 cup (1 stick) salted butter, softened to room temperature
1 tablespoon parsley leaves (finely chopped)
1 tablespoon basil leaves (finely chopped)
1 tablespoon chives (finely chopped)
1/4 teaspoon lemon zest

DIRECTIONS

Combine all the ingredients in a mini food processor. Once combined, transfer the herbed butter into a container where you can cover and store in the refrigerator. Refrigerate for at least 4 hours and up to about a month and use it as desired on breads, steamed vegetables, potatoes, or drizzle on meats. May also be formed into a roll using wax paper and stored in freezer.

Maple Butter

2 sticks (1 cup) real butter (softened to room temperature)
1/4 cup real maple syrup
1/2 cup brown sugar
1 teaspoon cinnamon

DIRECTIONS

In medium bowl, mix together all ingredients until well blended. Chill in refrigerator for about 30 minutes. Form into a roll using wax paper and store wrapped. Best used within 4 weeks. May also be frozen.

Rosemary and Garlic Butter

2 sprigs fresh rosemary
2 cloves garlic (finely minced)
1 teaspoon summer savory
Pinch sea salt
2 sticks (1 cup) unsalted butter,
    softened to room temperature

DIRECTIONS

Remove rosemary leaves from stalk by running your thumb and forefinger down the length of the stalk. Combine the rosemary, garlic, savory, and salt in a small mortar bowl and bash with the pestle until well mixed. Combine this mixture with the softened butter in a medium mixing bowl and blend thoroughly. Place on wax paper and form into a roll and chill. Great on beef, bread, and pasta. Store in refrigerator for up to 4 weeks. May also be frozen.

Notes

DRESSINGS, SAUCES, PESTO, AND DIPS

Cilantro Avocado Dressing

1 large avocado (chopped)
1 tablespoon avocado oil
2 tablespoons white balsamic vinegar
1 garlic clove (peeled)
1/2 teaspoon cumin powder
1 tablespoon cilantro
1 tablespoon red onion (chopped)
1 tablespoon fresh squeezed lime juice
1 teaspoon lime zest
4 tablespoons Greek yogurt or sour cream
1 teaspoon chili powder
1 teaspoon jalapeño (diced)
1 tablespoon green onion or chives (chopped)
Sea salt to taste
White pepper to taste

DIRECTIONS

In blender, combine all ingredients except salt and pepper and blend until creamy. Add salt and pepper to taste.

Notes

Jalapeño Vinaigrette

1/4 cup balsamic vinegar
4 tablespoons olive oil
1 clove garlic (minced)
3 fresh basil leaves (finely chopped)
*4 tablespoons honey
*1 teaspoon chopped jalapeño

DIRECTIONS

Mix all ingredients well. Refrigerate or let stand for 10 to 15 minutes. Enjoy as a dressing on tossed salad. Use immediately or keep refrigerated up to 3 days. You may also use it as a glaze when baking or grilling meats—just add equal parts olive oil and the dressing for baking or grilling.

*You may substitute 5 tablespoons jalapeño jelly for the honey and fresh chopped jalapeños.

Lemon-Dijon Vinaigrette Dressing

1/4 cup olive oil
3 tablespoons fresh lemon juice
1 teaspoon Dijon mustard
3/4 teaspoon sugar
1/2 teaspoon salt
1/4 teaspoon pepper

DIRECTIONS

Whisk together all ingredients. Toss over your favorite salad. Use immediately or keep refrigerated up to 3 days.

Notes

Lemony Dill Dressing

3 tablespoons extra-virgin olive oil
2 tablespoons fresh lemon juice
2 tablespoon fresh dill (finely chopped)
Sea salt and freshly ground pepper

DIRECTIONS

In a large bowl, whisk the olive oil with the lemon juice and dill and season with salt and pepper. Use immediately or keep refrigerated up to 3 days.

Tarragon-Mustard Vinaigrette

1 tablespoon fresh lemon juice
1 tablespoon Dijon mustard
1/2 teaspoon salt
3 tablespoons olive oil
*2 tablespoons fresh tarragon (finely chopped)

DIRECTIONS

Whisk together first three ingredients in small bowl until well blended. Add oil slowly and continue whisking. Stir in tarragon. Use immediately or keep refrigerated up to 3 days.

*Fresh basil or flat-leaf parsley may be substituted for the tarragon if desired.

Notes

Raspberry Salad Dressing

1/4 cup white wine vinegar
2 tablespoons raspberries (mashed)
1 tablespoon honey
1/2 cup olive oil

DIRECTIONS

Whisk together first 3 ingredients in a bowl until blended. Slowly add olive oil, whisking constantly until thoroughly blended. Use immediately or keep refrigerated up to 3 days.

Citrus Cumin Dressing

3 tablespoons fresh orange juice
2 tablespoons fresh lemon juice
1/2 teaspoon sugar
1/2 teaspoon cumin
1/4 teaspoon salt
1/4 teaspoon white pepper
1/3 cup olive oil

DIRECTIONS

Whisk together first 6 ingredients in small bowl. Add oil slowly and continue to whisk until well blended. Use immediately or keep refrigerated up to 3 days.

Notes

Citrus Vinaigrette

- 1/3 cup grapeseed oil
- 1/4 cup honey
- 4 teaspoons lime zest
- 6 tablespoons fresh squeezed lime juice
- 2 tablespoons fresh orange juice

DIRECTIONS

In small bowl, whisk all ingredients together until well blended. Serve immediately over your favorite salad.

Tomato Basil Vinaigrette

- 1-1/4 to 1-1/2 pounds fresh tomatoes (seeded and diced)
- 2 medium shallots (thinly sliced)
- 1/4 cup lightly packed basil
- 1/3 cup red wine vinegar
- 3/4 cup olive oil
- Sea salt
- Black pepper

DIRECTIONS

In medium bowl, gently mix all ingredients except salt and pepper. Add salt and pepper to taste. Set aside at room temperature until serving time. Great topping for steak.

Notes

Lemon Garlic Olive Oil

1/3 cup fresh squeezed lemon juice
4 teaspoons lemon zest
3 cloves garlic (minced)
1/4 teaspoon salt
1/4 teaspoon white pepper
1/2 cup olive oil
1/2 cup sour cream

DIRECTIONS

Combine all ingredients except sour cream in blender and puree. Transfer to bowl and whisk in sour cream. Transfer to container and refrigerate for at least 15 minutes before serving.

Not Your Granny's Cranberry Sauce

2 cups sugar
4 cups fresh cranberries
3/4 cup water
1/4 cup orange juice
1/2 cup port wine

DIRECTIONS

Stir together sugar, port wine, and 3/4 cup water in heavy saucepan until blended. Add cranberries, bring to boil, cooking evenly over medium high heat, stirring often, 8-10 minutes or until cranberry skins start to split. Remove from heat and allow to cool. Pour mixture into blender and pulse 3-4 times until almost pureed, stir in orange juice. Cover and chill 8 hours before serving. Can be stored in tight container for up to 2 weeks.

Notes

Cilantro Pesto

1/2 cup fresh cilantro leaves
1/2 cup fresh flat leaf parsley
2 garlic cloves
1/4 cup Parmesan cheese (freshly grated)
2 tablespoons pumpkin seeds (toasted)
1/4 teaspoon salt
1/4 cup olive oil

DIRECTIONS

Pulse the first 6 ingredients in food processor until chopped. Slowly drizzle olive oil in and continue to pulse until a coarse mixture forms. Cover and chill until ready to serve. Keep refrigerated up to 1 week.

Pecan Pesto

1-1/2 cups basil leaves
3/4 cup pecan oil
3/4 cup pecan pieces
1 clove garlic
1 teaspoon salt
1 teaspoon black pepper

DIRECTIONS

Place basil and pecan oil in blender, pulse until basil is finely chopped. Add the remaining ingredients. Pulse until pecans are ground and mixture is well combined. Store in refrigerator up to 1 week or freeze.

Notes

Tropical Tzatziki Sauce

1/2 English cucumber (finely chopped)
*1-1/2 cups plain coconut yogurt
2 garlic cloves (minced)
1 teaspoon lemon zest
1 tablespoon freshly-squeezed
    lemon juice
3 tablespoons dill (finely chopped)
Pinch of salt
*Plain yogurt may be substituted for
    the coconut yogurt.

DIRECTIONS

In a mixing bowl, combine the yogurt, olive oil, lemon juice, salt, pepper, dill, and garlic. Blend thoroughly and serve. Can be stored in tight container up to 3 days.

Easy Breezy Honey Mustard Dipping Sauce

1-1/2 cups mayonnaise or plain Greek yogurt
1/4 cup Dijon mustard
1/2 cup honey

DIRECTIONS

Blend together all ingredients until well blended. Great dipping sauce for chicken tenders or fried shrimp. Store in tight container in refrigerator up to 2 weeks.

Sweet Corn and Black Bean Salsa

1 can (15 oz.) black beans (rinsed and drained)
1 can (15 oz.) sweet corn (drained and rinsed)
1 tablespoon jalapeño pepper (finely chopped)
1 large tomato (chopped)
1/4 cup finely sweet onion (chopped)
2 tablespoons cilantro (finely chopped)
1 teaspoon cumin powder
1 teaspoon chili powder
1 teaspoon lime juice
Salt to taste
1 large avocado (cut into cubes)
Sour cream

DIRECTIONS

Toss all ingredients (except avocado and sour cream) together in large bowl. Refrigerate for 1 hour. Top with chopped avocado and dollop of sour cream and serve with chips or use as a topping for tacos.

Notes

Mango-Corn Salsa

1 ripe mango (diced)
1 medium lime (juiced)
*2 fresh ears of corn on the cob
    (grilled and kernels scraped off)*
2 tablespoons of fresh cilantro
    (chopped)
1/2 cup of red onion (chopped)
1 teaspoon of Tajin seasoning
*1 cup cooked frozen corn or canned
    corn may be substituted*

DIRECTIONS

Mix all ingredients together except lime juice and Tajin. Gently toss, mixing well.
Add lime juice and Tajin and toss again. Chill at least 1 hour before serving.

Notes

Herb and Bleu Cheese Toppers

1 dozen paper baking cups
Cooking spray
2 packages cream cheese
    (8 oz.) at room temperature
1/2 cup sour cream
4 oz. bleu cheese (crumbled)
1 tablespoon flour
1 teaspoon Mediterranean dried seasoning mix (without salt)
1 clove garlic (finely minced)
2 large eggs

DIRECTIONS

Preheat the oven to 325°F. Place paper baking cups into a muffin pan and spray with cooking spray. Beat all remaining ingredients together with electric blender until well blended. Spoon into baking cups and bake for 40 minutes or until set. Allow them to cool completely, then refrigerate for at least 4 hours. Remove from paper cups and use as a topper for salads, spread on warm bread, or as a dip. Keep refrigerated for up to 1 week or freeze. If frozen, allow them to completely thaw before use.

Green Chutney

1 bunch fresh mint
1 bunch fresh cilantro
1 jalapeño (seeds and stem removed)
1/4 cup water
2 tablespoons fresh lime juice
1 tablespoon sea salt
1/2 teaspoon ground cumin

DIRECTIONS

Combine mint, cilantro, jalapeño, 1/4 cup water, lime juice, 1 teaspoon salt, and cumin in a blender. Process until smooth. Refrigerate chutney in an airtight container and chill until ready to serve.

Creamy Zesty Spinach Artichoke Dip

14 oz. canned artichoke hearts
 (drained, chopped)
1 bag (10-oz.) frozen spinach
 (chopped, thawed and drained)
8 oz. cream cheese
1 cup Parmesan cheese (grated)
1 cup Mozzarella cheese (grated)
4 garlic cloves (minced)
1/2 teaspoon white pepper
1 teaspoon red pepper flakes

DIRECTIONS

Heat the cream cheese in a small bowl in the microwave set on high for 1 minute.
Add the spinach and artichoke hearts to the cream cheese and stir well. Add the
remaining ingredients to the cream cheese and combine. Serve hot with crackers,
chips, or toasted bread for dipping.

Notes

SALADS

Kicking Jalapeño Coleslaw

1 (16 oz.) bag shredded coleslaw
1 or 2 small jalapeño peppers (seeded and thinly sliced)
1 cup red onion (thinly-sliced)
1/4 cup green onion (chopped)

Dressing:

1/4 cup mayonnaise
2 tablespoons sugar
2 tablespoons mustard
1 tablespoon apple cider vinegar
1 teaspoon salt
1/2 teaspoon black pepper
1/4 teaspoon ground cumin

DIRECTIONS

In a large bowl, stir together coleslaw, jalapeño, red onion, and green onions. In a small bowl, whisk together the dressing mixture of mayonnaise, sugar, mustard, vinegar, salt, pepper, and cumin until smooth. Add the dressing to the large bowl of coleslaw mixture and toss until it is thoroughly coated. Cover and refrigerate for at least 1 hour.

Notes

Garlicky-Minty-Basil Bowtie Pasta

1 bag (16 oz.) pasta (bowtie or
    penne)
2 large garlic cloves (diced)
2 tablespoons mint
    (cut into ribbons)
2 tablespoons basil
    (cut into ribbons)
2 tablespoons chives (chopped)
3 tablespoons lemon juice
6 tablespoons good olive oil
Salt and pepper to taste

DIRECTIONS

Prepare pasta according to directions on bag. In a small bowl, mix garlic, mint, basil, lemon juice, and 3 tablespoons of the olive oil while pasta is cooking. Drain pasta, rinse with cold water and pour into large bowl. Stir in the remaining 3 tablespoons of the olive oil and allow pasta to cool. Once cooled, pour in the mixture from the small bowl and gently toss until well mixed. Add salt and pepper to taste. Let refrigerate for at least one hour before serving.

Notes

Triple A Green Apple Salad

1(16 oz.) bag fresh arugula
1 small green apple (cut into cubes)
1 celery stalk (diced)
1 medium shallot bulb (thinly sliced)
1/4 cup parsley (chopped)
1/2 English cucumber (diced)
4 tablespoons fresh-squeezed
    lemon juice
8 tablespoons good extra virgin olive oil
Salt
Fresh ground black pepper
1/4 cup Parmesan cheese
2 tablespoons roasted salted pumpkin seeds
1 medium avocado (cubed)

DIRECTIONS

In a large bowl, mix the arugula, apple, celery, shallot, parley, and cucumber. Wisk together the lemon juice and olive oil and pour over the salad mix. Add salt and fresh ground black pepper to taste. Top with avocado cubes and sprinkle with Parmesan cheese and pumpkin seeds.

Notes

Cool-n-Spicy Shrimp Salad

2 bags boil-n-bag rice
Liquid Shrimp Boil
    (such as Zatarain's)
1/2 cup green olives (chopped)
1/3 cup onion (chopped)
1 cup mayonnaise
1 pound (peeled and deveined
    raw shrimp)
Lettuce leaves
Avocado slices
Tomato wedges

DIRECTIONS

Bring 6 cups of water to boil in a large pot. Add 2 tablespoons of liquid shrimp boil and the raw shrimp. Cook for about 2 minutes until shrimp is firm. Remove the shrimp from water and allow to cool—but do not pour out the water. Return the water to boil, add the boil-n-bag rice and boil according to the instructions. Chop the shrimp and combine it with olive, onion and mayonnaise. Once rice is done, allow to cool before adding it to the shrimp mixture. Stir together all ingredients. Allow to cool for at least 1 hour. Add salt and pepper to taste. Serve atop lettuce and garnished with avocado and tomato wedges. Or serve stuffed into hollowed-out tomatoes.

Notes

Summer Pasta Salad

3 medium red, ripe heirloom tomatoes (chopped)
1/4 cup shallots (chopped)
1 tablespoon balsamic vinegar
6 tablespoons extra virgin olive oil
1/4 cup loosely packed fresh basil (chopped)
1 lb. cavatappi pasta
1/2 cup feta cheese
Sea salt
Freshly ground black pepper

DIRECTIONS

Cook the pasta in a large pot according to directions. Gently mix chopped tomatoes, shallots, and basil in large bowl. When the pasta is done, drain it thoroughly and add it to the bowl. Gently fold olive oil and feta cheese into the salad mixture, adding salt and pepper to taste. Let the salad sit for 5 minutes before serving, folding gently a couple of times to distribute the tomato juices and olive oil.

Notes

Tuna Niçoise Salad

(1) 12 oz. can albacore tuna packed in water
(1) 10.5 oz. bag steamable frozen whole
    green beans
(1) 1.5-lb. bag medley petite new potato
4 boiled eggs (sliced in half)
15 oz. bag mixed salad greens
12 grape tomatoes
12 black olives
1 large lemon (sliced into wedges)
1/2 cup flat leaf parsley (chopped)
2 tablespoons olive oil
Sea salt
Black pepper

DIRECTIONS

Preheat the oven to 450°F. Wash and cut potatoes in half lengthwise. Toss potatoes in olive oil and sprinkle with salt and pepper. Arrange on baking sheet in single layer. Roast until tender. Steam green beans according to directions. Drain tuna and set aside. Assemble salad greens on large platter as the base of the salad and arrange all remaining ingredients for presentation. Top off individual servings with your favorite vinaigrette dressing.

Notes

Cool Cucumber and Watermelon Salad

- 1 large English cucumber (diced)
- 2 cups watermelon (seeded and diced)
- 1/2 cup red onion (thinly sliced)
- 1 cup Citrus Vinaigrette
- 1 tablespoon fresh mint (finely chopped)
- Salt and pepper to taste

DIRECTIONS

Mix all ingredients in large bowl. Chill for at least 1 hour before serving.

Creamy Cucumber Salad

- 2 lbs. English cucumbers
  (peeled and thinly sliced crosswise)
- *1/4 cup sour cream*
- 1 tablespoon apple cider vinegar
- 1 tablespoon olive oil
- 1 teaspoon Dijon mustard
- 1 small red onion, halved and thinly sliced
- 1/4 cup fresh dill (chopped)
- Salt
- Freshly ground black pepper
- *substitute plain non-fat yogurt for a lighter version if desired*

DIRECTIONS

Place the cucumbers in a large colander and toss with a couple of large pinches of salt. Set the colander in a large bowl or in the sink and let the cucumbers stand 30 minutes at room temperature to release some of their water. Meanwhile, whisk the sour cream, vinegar, oil, mustard, a pinch of salt, and a few grinds of pepper together in a large bowl; set aside. Gently pat the cucumbers dry with a paper towel. Add the cucumbers, red onion, and dill to the dressing and toss gently to combine. Taste and season with more salt and pepper as needed.

Heirloom Tomatoes and Cucumber Salad

3 large Heirloom tomatoes that have not been refrigerated for best taste (rough cut)

1 medium English Cucumber (sliced)

1 medium shallot bulb (thinly sliced)

3 stalks celery (sliced)

1/2 small green bell pepper (sliced)

1/2 small red bell pepper (sliced)

3/4 cup olive oil

1/4 cup white balsamic vinegar

1/2 tablespoon sugar

Sea salt to taste

White pepper to taste

DIRECTIONS

Combine all ingredients in large bowl. Mix well. Best served immediately at room temperature.

Notes

Strawberries and Field Greens Salad

12 large strawberries (sliced)
6 cups mixed field greens
1 medium shallot (thinly sliced)
1/4 cup citrus flavored rice vinegar
1/2 cup avocado oil
Sea salt to taste
Black pepper to taste

DIRECTIONS

Combine strawberries, greens, and shallot in large bowl. Toss well. Plate for individual servings. Mix oil and vinegar, adding salt and pepper to taste. Use desired amount of dressing on each serving.

Notes

Rainbow Kale Salad

1 bunch dinosaur kale
    (thinly sliced into ribbons)
1-pint cherry tomatoes, mixed color (sliced in half)
1/4 cup red onion (thinly sliced)
1/4 cup lemon juice
3/4 cup olive oil
1 tablespoon red pepper flakes
Sea salt
Black pepper

DIRECTIONS

Mix all kale, tomatoes, and red onions in large bowl. Mix oil and vinegar stirring well. Pour about half the mixture over the salad, toss well. Cover and chill overnight. Before serving, sprinkle with red pepper flakes and add salt and pepper to taste. Add additional dressing as desired.

Tropical Fruit with Rose Water Vinaigrette

4 cups fresh mixed tropical fruit
   (cubed)
2 tablespoons mint (chopped)
3 tablespoons honey
1 tablespoon lime juice
2 tablespoons rose water
Mint sprigs for garnish
1 tablespoon edible rose petals for garnish (optional)

DIRECTIONS

Mix all fruit in a large bowl. Mix mint, honey, lime juice, and rose water in small bowl and stir until well combined. Pour over fruit and garnish with fresh mint and edible rose petals.

Notes

Taco Tuesday Salad

(1) 15 oz. can black beans
1 15 oz can corn kernels
2 tomatoes (diced)
1/2 head lettuce (shredded)
1 lb. of chicken breast
1 lb. ground beef
1/2 cup Mexican cheese
1/4 cup jalapeños
    (sliced fresh or canned)
1 bag taco seasoning

DIRECTIONS

Cook the ground beef and chicken per the taco seasoning instructions in separate pans. Warm the beans and corn in separate pans; drain. Use a large platter to line up the salad, keeping the meats to the outside and positioning the vegetables on the inside. Spread the jalapeños and cheese to one end. Serve with Cilantro Avocado Dressing.

Notes

ENTREES

Herbed T-Bone Steak

1 T-bone steak
1 tablespoon Italian seasoning
2 tablespoons olive oil
2 rosemary sprigs
Coarsely ground black pepper
Salt to taste

DIRECTIONS

Rub steak with salt and pepper. Massage in Italian seasoning. Thread rosemary leaves from the stalk and poke rosemary stalks into meat. Let stand for 30 minutes. Heat oil in a skillet over high heat and sear steak on both sides, then turn and cook on each side about 2 minutes. Continue until desired doneness is achieved. Remove rosemary stalks. Let steak rest for 5 minutes before serving. Great with Herbed Butter.

Notes

Napa Cabbage Rolls

1 large head Napa cabbage
1 lb. ground beef
1 lb. ground lamb
1/4 cup mayonnaise
2 tablespoons garlic (minced)
1/2 cup onions (chopped)
1/2 cup green bell pepper (chopped)
1/2 cup precooked brown rice
1 egg
2 tablespoons Mediterranean or Italian seasoning
1/4 teaspoon black pepper
1 can (14.5 oz.) Italian stewed tomatoes (diced)
1 can (6 oz.) tomato paste
1/4 cup chicken broth
2 tablespoons butter

DIRECTIONS

Preheat the oven to 350°F. In a large mixing bowl, combine beef, lamb, mayonnaise, garlic, onions, green bell pepper, Mediterranean or Italian seasoning, and black pepper. Beat egg in a separate bowl and fold into the meat mixture. Add the rice and mix well. Tear off cabbage leaves and rinse well. Pat dry. Use your hands to form mounds of meat and place on a cabbage leaf. Roll leaf around the mound and secure with toothpick. Repeat until all meat is used. Mix chicken broth, tomato paste and stewed tomatoes. Pour about 1 cup into large baking pan. Place rolls atop the sauce in the pan. Bake until the meat is thoroughly done, about 40 minutes. Simmer then pour the remaining sauce atop cabbage rolls to serve.

Notes

Lime Marinated Grilled Chicken Salad

Juice of 1 lime
2 boneless chicken breasts
2 tablespoons olive oil
Cayenne pepper
1 tablespoon creole seasoning
1 medium yellow squash (sliced)
1 cucumber (sliced)
1 orange bell pepper (sliced)
1 head lettuce (shredded)

DIRECTIONS

Place clean chicken breasts in sealable container and coat with 1 tablespoon olive oil on both sides. Pour lime juice over chicken. Sprinkle cayenne pepper to taste and creole seasoning on both sides of chicken. Allow to marinate 3-4 hours. Grill chicken on each side for about 10 minutes total, or until done. Allow to cool, and slice into strips about 1/2-inch thick. Coat squash and bell peppers in remaining olive oil. Grill vegetables on both sides until tender. Place lettuce and cucumber on platter. Top with grilled chicken and grilled vegetables. Serve with a citrus-based dressing.

Notes

Grilled Packs

1 lb. of new potatoes – red or yellow (quartered)
12 corn on the cob mini ears
(or 6 ears cut in half)
4 spicy link sausages (sliced 1/4 inch thick)
Mushrooms (sliced in half)
1/2 stick of butter (cut into 6 equal parts)
1 bell pepper – red or orange (sliced)
Tajin seasoning
Salt
Pepper
12 ice cubes
6 sheets of foil paper (each approximately 8 inches square)

DIRECTIONS

Place an equal amount of each ingredient on the foil sheets. Add 2 ice cubes and a slice of butter to each foil. Season each with Tajin or salt and pepper to taste. Seal tightly on all sides (the ice will steam cook along with the butter). Place on heated grill for 15-20 minutes, being careful not to burn the pack. Remove from grill and open carefully to release steam before serving.

Beefy Fajita Lettuce Wraps

2 tablespoons olive oil
1 cup sliced red onion (shredded)
1-1/2 cups yellow, red, and green bell pepper (seeded and sliced)
1 lb. precooked, preseasoned beef fajita in bag
1 teaspoon cumin
1 teaspoon garlic powder
1 teaspoon chili powder
1 lime, juiced
2 tablespoons fresh cilantro
12 butter lettuce leaves
Garnish: chopped or sliced avocado, fresh cilantro sprigs,
    sliced limes, and 1 small container (8 oz.) of premade pico de gallo.

DIRECTIONS

In a large saucepan, heat oil over medium heat and add onion and bell peppers. Cook until tender. Add thawed beef fajita meat and stir until meat is evenly heated throughout. Add a dash of ground cumin, garlic powder, and chili powder to taste. Remove from heat and stir in lime juice. Let the mixture to rest for about 5 minutes. Stir in cilantro. Using a slotted spoon, spoon beef fajita and vegetable mixture into center of each lettuce leaf. Garnish each leaf with chopped or sliced avocado, fresh cilantro, a slice of lime, and about 1 tablespoon of pico de gallo.

Notes

Shrimp Scampi

1 lb. large shrimp (peeled and deveined)
1 (12 oz.) package angel hair pasta
1/3 cup butter
1/4 cup finely chopped sweet onion
3 garlic cloves (finely chopped)
1 tablespoon Italian herb seasoning
1 teaspoon Worcestershire sauce
2 tablespoons lemon juice
1/4 cup romano or Parmesan cheese
1 tablespoon parsley (chopped)

DIRECTIONS

Prepare angel hair pasta according to directions on package. Melt butter in a large skillet over medium high heat, add onion and garlic, and sauté for about 3-5 minutes, or until tender. Stir in Italian seasoning and Worcestershire sauce. Reduce heat to medium and add shrimp. Stir occasionally, 3-5 minutes until the shrimp turn pink. Stir in lemon juice. Toss shrimp mixture into pasta, sprinkle with cheese and parsley. Serve immediately.

Notes

Jerked Shrimp-and-Savory Sweet Potatoes

1 lb. raw shrimp (deveined and peeled)
3 lbs. sweet potatoes
1/4 cup half-and-half
3 tablespoons butter
6 slices bacon
1 (8 oz.) package mushrooms (sliced)
1/4 cup red bell pepper (diced)
1/4 cup yellow onion (diced)
1 teaspoon dry Caribbean seasoning mix
4 oz. chicken broth
Caribbean Jerk seasoning
Lemon juice
Fresh parsley sprigs or chives (for topping)

DIRECTIONS

Fry bacon slices. Remove bacon and drain on paper towel. Sauté peppers and onions in the bacon drippings on medium heat until onions begin to turn translucent. Add mushrooms and shrimp, adding jerk seasoning to taste. Cook until shrimp turns pink. Remove from heat and place in bowl, stir in lemon juice, chicken broth, and 2 tablespoons half-and-half. Peel sweet potatoes, pierce with fork, and microwave until tender, about 10-12 minutes. Let cool, cut into chunks and place into a large bowl. Add butter, Caribbean seasoning, and remaining half-and-half. Mash the potatoes until smooth. Spoon sweet potato mixture onto plate and top with the shrimp mixture. Sprinkle with parsley or chive topping.

Notes

Mixed Grill

4 (1-1/2-inch thick) center cut pork chops
4 (6 oz.) beef tenderloin fillets
    (about 2 inches thick)
Salt
Pepper
Rosemary sprigs
Chives
Cilantro sprigs

DIRECTIONS

Sprinkle pork chops and beef with desired amount of salt and pepper. Grill over medium high heat about 8-10 minutes on each side. Cook in additional 5-minute intervals, on each side, until desired degree of doneness. Remove chops and beef from grill and allow to rest for 5 minutes. Serve with Cilantro Pesto and garnish with rosemary, chives, and cilantro.

Notes

Mexico City Shrimp and Angel Hair Pasta

2 dozen large shrimp (deveined and peeled)
18 oz. refrigerated angel hair pasta
1 jar (8 oz.) adobo Mexican sauce
1 small can (7 oz.) Chipotle chilis in adobo sauce
5 tablespoons fresh squeezed lime juice
1 tablespoon minced garlic
1/4 cup chopped onion
Lime wedges
Toppings: Parmesan cheese, chives, cilantro

DIRECTIONS

Remove Chipotle chilis from can and set aside. These are hot. Mix the sauces together. Use 1/4 cup of adobo sauce combined with the lime juice as a marinade for shrimp. Toss shrimp in marinade, let stand for up to 30 minutes, then cook shrimp on the grill until shrimp turns pink. Discard sauce used for marinade. Cook angel hair pasta according to the directions. Sautee onions and garlic on low heat and add the remaining sauce once onions begin to caramelize. Add remaining adobo sauce and simmer. Toss adobo sauce and pasta, coating the pasta. Serve with desired amount of shrimp on each plate. Squeeze lime juice over the pasta and top off with Parmesan cheese, cilantro, and chives according to taste.

Notes

Miss Bea's Shrimp & Cheese Corn Grits

1 lb. shrimp
  (raw, deveined, and tails off)
1 link andouille sausage (sliced)
1 link jalapeño sausage (sliced)
6 strips bacon
1 stick unsalted butter
1 tablespoon plus 1 teaspoon all-purpose flour
2 green bell peppers, cut lengthwise into 1/4-inch-thick slices
1 large onion, halved lengthwise and cut into 1/4-inch-thick slices
2 celery stalks, cut into 1/2-inch-thick pieces
2 tablespoons garlic (finely chopped)
2 cans stewed tomatoes
1 cup chicken broth
1/2 cup heavy cream
1 tablespoon Cajun seasoning
2 tablespoons gumbo file`

DIRECTIONS

Using a 3-inch deep frying pan, fry bacon until crisp. Remove bacon and place on paper towel to absorb excess liquid fat. In remaining bacon drippings, fry sausage on medium heat until evenly browned. Remove sausage. Add butter. Once butter is melted, add Cajun seasoning, bell peppers, onion, celery, and sauté until tender. Add garlic. Reduce heat and allow to simmer. Sprinkle in flour and mix well. Once the mixture begins to thicken, add chicken broth, stewed tomatoes, and gumbo file`. Continue to simmer and stir in heavy cream. Add shrimp and cook for about 3 minutes with lid on pan. If mixture is too thick, add additional chicken broth, 2 tablespoons at a time to create a smoother consistency. Turn off heat and keep pan covered.

Notes

Cheese Corn Grits

1 cup heavy cream
1 cup chicken broth
1/2 cup (1 stick) butter
1 cup uncooked grits
1 teaspoon salt
1/2 teaspoon white pepper
1 cup sharp Cheddar cheese (shredded)
1/2 cup Parmesan Cheese
1 cup fresh or frozen sweet corn
1/3 cup butter
1 tablespoon Cajun seasoning
Parsley and lemon wedges (for garnish)

DIRECTIONS

Preheat the oven to 350°F. Lightly grease a medium baking dish. Bring the milk and chicken broth to a boil in a pot over medium heat. Melt 1/2 cup butter in the boiling liquid. Gradually mix in the grits and cook 5 minutes, stirring constantly. Remove from heat and season with salt and pepper. Beat with a whisk or electric mixer until smooth. Add additional chicken broth 2 tablespoons at a time if mixture is too thick. Mix in the Cajun seasoning, corn, Cheddar cheese and 1/3 cup butter. Transfer to the prepared baking dish, and sprinkle with Parmesan cheese. Bake 1 hour in the preheated oven, until firm. Plate desired amount of Cheesy Corn Grits and top with shrimp and sausage mixture. Garnish with parsley and lemon wedge and serve immediately.

Notes

Mediterranean Lamb Chops

1/4 cup Mediterranean
    seasoning mix
4 French Rib lamb chops
Olive oil
Salt and pepper to taste

DIRECTIONS

Rub olive oil over lamb chops. Gently rub Mediterranean seasoning onto lamb chops and let sit overnight for best results. Prepare on grill, turning every 2 minutes until desired wellness.

Notes

Sweet and Savory Salmon

1 4-oz. salmon filet (skin on)
1 teaspoon cumin
1 tablespoon ancho chili powder
1 tablespoon brown sugar
1 teaspoon Cajun seasoning
1 tablespoon olive oil
Salt and pepper to taste

DIRECTIONS

Mix all seasoning together well in a small bowl. Gently rub salmon with seasoning and let rest for about 10 minutes. Place olive oil in pan and heat on medium high heat. Place salmon in pan, skin side up and cook for about 3 minutes until crisp on edges. Remove from heat and allow to rest for a few minutes before serving.

Notes

Dill Salmon

1 large salmon (whole fish or half)
1/2 tablespoon dill weed
1/2 tablespoon dill seed
1 teaspoon lemon pepper
1 teaspoon red pepper
1/2 teaspoon Tajin seasoning
1 tablespoon Hellmann's
    mayonnaise

DIRECTIONS

Preheat the oven at 400°F. Lightly coat cookie sheet with olive oil. Lay salmon evenly on the cookie sheet. Add thin layer of mayonnaise over the entire fish, including sides. Mix peppers and Tajin, and evenly sprinkle over fish. Mix dill weed and seed together and evenly sprinkle over entire fish. Place in oven and cook for 15 -20 minutes.

Bahamian Fried Snapper

1 Whole snapper
Pinch of salt
Dash of pepper
1 Lime
Flour (optional)
Vegetable/canola oil

DIRECTIONS

Score the skin on both sides of fish (cut from head to tail). Salt and pepper each side and squeeze lime on both sides. Marinate fish for an hour or overnight. Flour each side just before frying (optional). Heat oil in deep fryer or frying pan (enough oil to cover the sides of the fish.) Cook 6-7 minutes per side.

Notes

SOUPS & STEWS

Chicken Chili

(2) 14.5 oz. cans white beans
(1) 6 oz. can tomatillo sauce
1 tablespoon avocado oil
1 medium jalapeño pepper (minced)
2 medium poblano peppers (chopped)
1 large yellow onion (chopped)
4 garlic cloves (minced)
Salt and freshly ground black pepper
1 tablespoon ground cumin
1 1/2 teaspoons Mexican oregano
1 teaspoon ancho chili powder
4 cups low-sodium chicken broth
2 tablespoons freshly squeezed lime juice
1/4 cup fresh cilantro (chopped)
*2 cups precooked shredded chicken
Sour cream
Cilantro springs (for garnish)
*Cooked ground turkey may be substituted

DIRECTIONS

Drain and rinse canned beans. In medium bowl, mash half of the beans with fork
or potato masher until chunky. In Dutch oven, heat oil and sauté onions, peppers
and garlic about 5 minutes over medium heat. Add cumin, oregano, tomatillos, chili
powder and sauté for an additional minute. Add chicken stock, lime juice, and whole
and smashed beans. Stir in chicken and cilantro and simmer for 20 minutes. Add salt
and pepper to taste. Serve with a dollop of sour cream and cilantro sprig.

Notes

South of the Border Chicken Soup

2/3 cup brown rice
1 whole skinless (bone-in) chicken breast
    (about 1-1/2 lbs.)
1/2 cup onion (thinly sliced)
2 garlic cloves (smashed)
2 ears of shucked sweet corn cut into 6 pieces
    (frozen corn on the cob may be substituted)
1/2 teaspoon cumin
1/2 cup cilantro (chopped)
10 cups chicken broth
Fresh ground pepper
Salt
1 avocado (diced)
1/4 cup sour cream or plain yogurt
1 tablespoon drained small capers
1 cup yellow potatoes (cut into chunks)

DIRECTIONS

In large saucepan, combine the chicken, onions, garlic, corn, cumin, and 1/2 cup of cilantro with chicken broth. Season with salt and pepper and bring to boil. Simmer until chicken breast is cooked through, about 12-15 minutes. Add potatoes and rice to broth. Raise heat slightly to cook the potatoes and rice for about 8 minutes. Transfer the chicken to plate, allow to cool. Once cooled, pull the meat off the bones and shred. Return the chicken to the broth mixture, cook until potatoes are tender, and rice is cooked. Stir and ladle soup into bowls, top with dollop of sour cream, cilantro sprigs, a few capers, and avocado.

Notes

Kale and Sweet Potato Soup

2 tablespoons olive oil
1 medium yellow onion (roughly chopped about 2 cups)
1 cup red bell pepper (chopped)
4 garlic gloves (crushed)
1 teaspoon turmeric
1 Cajun seasoning
1 medium sweet potato (chopped)
1 bunch dinosaur kale (chopped)
4 cups chicken stock

DIRECTIONS

Heat olive oil in a large saucepan over medium heat. Add onion, red bell pepper, and garlic, and cook, stirring often. Stir in turmeric and Cajun seasoning and cook for about 2 minutes, stirring often. Add small amount of additional oil if needed. Add broth, bring to simmer. Add kale and potatoes. Cook until tender. Ladle into bowl and enjoy with a slice of Heavenly Cornbread.

Notes

Tomato Soup and Grilled Cheese

1 tablespoon olive oil
1 cup carrot (chopped)
4 stalks celery (chopped)
1 small sweet yellow onion
    (chopped)
2 cloves garlic (minced)
4 cups chicken broth
1 pinch salt
Ground white pepper, to taste
1 can (14.5 oz.) Italian Stewed tomatoes
1 can (14.5 oz.) crushed tomatoes
3 tablespoons tomato paste
2 teaspoons Italian seasoning
1/4 cup unsalted butter
1/4 cup all-purpose flour
1 cup heavy cream
1 cup grated Parmesan cheese

DIRECTIONS

Heat oil and butter in a large pot and sauté carrots, celery, onion, and garlic. Add broth and stir. Add canned tomatoes, tomato paste, and Italian seasoning. Stir well. Remove about 2 cups of the stock and use immersion blender to blend. Return to pot and add flour, cheese, and heavy cream. Simmer for another 10 minutes. If liquid thickens too much, add additional broth 2 tablespoons at a time until desired consistency. Serve with Grilled Cheese.

Notes

Grilled Cheese

Sea salt
12 oz. bacon
8 slices bread (1/2" thick each)
1/2 cup mayonnaise
1/2 lb. sliced Gruyere cheese
1/2 lb. sliced Provolone cheese
1/4 lb. sliced Cheddar cheese

DIRECTIONS

Place bacon in an even layer in skillet and cook until crisp, about 3 minutes per side. Transfer bacon to paper towel-lined plate to drain. Spread each piece of bread with a thin layer of mayonnaise. Place bread in cast iron skillet, mayonnaise-side down, and cook on medium heat. Top bread with slices of Gruyere, Cheddar, and Provolone. When cheese has begun to melt, top with slice of bread that has been coated with mayonnaise. Place the mayonnaise side up. Flip occasionally until both sides are golden brown. Serve immediately.

Notes

Italian Sausage and Kale Soup

1 lb. hot Italian sausage
5 cups chicken stock
1 cup heavy cream
1 medium onion (chopped)
2 stalks celery (chopped)
1/4 cup red bell pepper
    (chopped)
1 bunch dinosaur kale (lower stems removed, chopped)
3 garlic cloves (minced)
4 large Yukon Gold potatoes (cut into large chunks)
2 tablespoons Italian seasoning
Salt and pepper to taste

DIRECTIONS

Heat 1 tablespoon olive oil in Dutch oven. Add crumbled Italian sausage, onions, celery, garlic, pepper, and Italian seasoning. Cook until meat is golden brown. Add chicken stock, kale, and potatoes. Bring to boil, reduce heat to medium, cover and cook for about 20 minutes, or until potatoes are tender. Add cream, stir well and simmer for 5 minutes.

Notes

Miss Helen's Ratatouille

2 tablespoons olive oil
1 large eggplant (diced into 1/2-inch chunks)
1 large yellow onion (chopped)
1 red bell pepper (sliced)
1 yellow bell pepper (sliced)
1 bay leaf
1 tablespoon tomato paste
1/2 cup dry white wine
1/4 cup chicken stock
1 zucchini (sliced into 1/4-inch-thick coins)
1 yellow squash (sliced into 1/4-inch-thick coins)
3 cloves garlic (minced)
2 cups Roma tomatoes (chopped)
1 teaspoon dried oregano
Kosher salt
Pinch of crushed red pepper flakes
Bunch of fresh basil
1/4 cup mascarpone cheese
Thick sliced whole wheat bread or any bread of your choice

DIRECTIONS

Place eggplant in a large bowl and toss with a big pinch of salt. Let sit for about 20 minutes, drain liquid and pat the eggplant dry. In Dutch oven, heat 1 tablespoon oil. Add eggplant and season with salt and pepper. Cook until golden all over and remove. Add remaining tablespoon of oil to pot. Add onion, bell peppers, and bay leaf and cook, stirring occasionally, until onion and peppers are beginning to turn tender, about 5 minutes. Add tomato paste and stir, then deglaze the pan with the white wine and chicken stock, reduce until most of the liquid has evaporated. Stir in zucchini and squash and cook until tender. Stir in garlic, tomatoes and oregano, red pepper flakes, salt and pepper and cook until the tomatoes start to break down. Continue to stir. Add the eggplant back to the pot and stir to combine. Garnish with basil, mascarpone cheese and serve with warm bread.

Notes

Grandma's Roasted Corn Chowder

6 slices bacon
1 large yellow onion (chopped)
1 lb. gold potatoes (diced)
1/4 cup carrots (shredded)
4 cups chicken broth
2 tablespoons flour
1/2 cup whole milk
4 ears of fresh corn
1/2 cup heavy cream
4 tablespoons Herbed Butter
1 cup white Cheddar cheese (shredded)
Kosher salt
Freshly ground black pepper
1 tablespoon chives (chopped, for garnish)

DIRECTIONS

Preheat the oven to 425°F. Rinse and clean the corn. Place each ear on a sheet of foil and coat with 1 tablespoon of Herbed Butter. Wrap corn and roast in oven for 20 minutes. Allow to cool and scrape the kernels into a bowl. In a large pot over medium heat, cook bacon until crisp. Remove bacon onto a paper-towel lined plate. Drain all but one tablespoon fat and cook the onions until translucent, about 4 minutes. Add potatoes, carrots and chicken stock and bring to a boil. Reduce heat, cover, and simmer for about 10 minutes, or until the potatoes are tender. In a bowl, whisk flour into milk, then stir that mixture into the pot. Add corn, cream, cheese, and bacon. Bring soup back to a boil, cooking until cheese is melted. Season with salt and pepper to taste and garnish with chives before serving.

Notes

Slow Cooker Green Chili Stew

1 lb. boneless pork loin (cubed)
1/2 cup flour
1-1/2 teaspoons olive oil
1/2 yellow onion (chopped)
1-3/4 cups fresh tomatoes (chopped)
1 cup diced green chile peppers
1 cup chicken broth
1-1/2 teaspoons ground cumin
1/2 large potato (cubed)
1-1/2 cloves garlic (minced)
1 teaspoon fresh cilantro (chopped)
1 teaspoon dried Mexican oregano
1/2 dash cayenne pepper
1 pinch salt to taste
1 pinch ground white pepper to taste
Sour cream

DIRECTIONS

Place the pork loin cubes and flour a plastic bag, and shake to coat the meat. Heat the olive oil in a large skillet over medium-high heat and cook and stir the meat cubes until evenly browned, about 10 minutes. Place the meat, onion, tomatoes, green chile peppers, chicken broth, cumin, potato, garlic, oregano, cilantro, cayenne pepper, salt, and white pepper in a slow cooker. Cook on low heat until the meat is tender, about 8 hours. Serve with a dollop of sour cream.

Notes

Beef Stew

3 cups mini potatoes (halved)
2 cups carrots (sliced)
1/2 cup celery (chopped)
1 small onion (sliced)
1/4 cup dried cremini mushrooms
3 bay leaves
1-1/2 lbs. beef stew meat
1/4 cup flour
1/4 teaspoon white pepper
1 tablespoon olive oil
2 cups chicken stock
2 tablespoons red wine
1 tablespoon Worcestershire sauce
1 tablespoon fresh thyme (chopped)
3 cloves garlic (minced)

DIRECTIONS

Combine vegetables in large slow cooker. Add bay leaves. Place beef, flour, and pepper into a sealable plastic bag and toss to coat beef. Heat oil in a large non-stick skillet. Brown beef well on all sides over medium-high heat. Place beef on top of vegetables in slow cooker. Sprinkle 1 teaspoon flour into the pan drippings and brown. Make sure to stir constantly with wooden spoon to keep it from burning. Add broth, wine, Worcestershire sauce, thyme and garlic to skillet and combine well with pan drippings. Pour mixture over beef and vegetables. Cover and cook on high setting for 4 hours or until the beef is fork tender. Discard bay leaves before serving.

Notes

Butternut Squash Soup

1 tablespoon olive oil
1 large onion, chopped
3 garlic cloves, minced
48 oz. butternut squash
    (frozen or fresh already cubed)
2 cups vegetable broth
2 cups chicken broth
3/4 teaspoon salt
1/4 teaspoon pepper
1/2 cup heavy whipping cream

DIRECTIONS

Heat the oil over medium heat in a large saucepan. Add the onion, then cook and stir until tender. Add the garlic and cook for 1 minute more. Add in the squash, broth, salt and pepper. Bring the mixture to a boil, then reduce heat and simmer, covered, until the squash is tender. This should take about 10 to 15 minutes. Once the squash is tender, use an immersion blender to puree soup in the pot. Or allow soup to cool and puree small batches in blender. Add the cream to pureed soup and simmer until heated. If your soup is looking a little thin after pureeing, whisk together two tablespoons of olive oil with two tablespoons of flour until smooth and add to soup and simmer until thickens to desired consistency.

Notes

Moroccan Chicken Tagine

2 preserved lemons
(quartered and seeds removed)
8 chicken thighs
2 large onions (finely chopped)
3 cloves garlic (minced)
1/4 cup fresh cilantro (chopped)
1/4 cup fresh parsley (chopped)
1 teaspoons ginger
1 teaspoon black pepper
1 teaspoon turmeric
1/2 teaspoon salt (or less, to taste)
1/3 cup olive oil
1/4 cup chicken stock
1/2 cup whole olives (green and red, for garnish)

DIRECTIONS

Remove the flesh from the preserved lemon and chop finely. Add the lemon to a bowl along with the chicken, onion, garlic, cilantro, parsley, ginger, pepper, turmeric, and salt. Mix well. Lightly salt chicken and let sit for a few minutes. Heat olive oil in a Dutch oven and brown the chicken. Add broth and add remaining mixture to Dutch oven. Cook on medium heat for 1 hour or until chicken is well done. Serve over rice or couscous. Add olives as garnish.

Notes

LITE BITES

Bruschetta with Olives

4 tablespoon extra-virgin olive oil
2 cloves garlic (minced)
4 Roma tomatoes (diced)
3 tablespoons basil (chopped)
4 tablespoon balsamic vinegar
1/4 tablespoon crushed red pepper flakes
Pinch kosher salt
1/4 cup chopped olives (optional)
1 French baguette

DIRECTIONS

Preheat the oven to 450°F. In bowl, mix 2 tablespoons of olive oil, garlic and add basil. Let stand 10 minutes. Add olives, tomatoes, and red peppers to mixture. Cut baguette into 1/4 slices and lay on baker's sheet Take the remaining olive oil and brush the top of baguette slices. Toast bread 7-9 minutes. Let bread cool for 5 minutes before topping with mixture. Add pinch of kosher salt and drizzle with balsamic vinegar. Serve immediately

Notes

Mamaw's Spiced Fried Wings

12 chicken wings
2 eggs
1 tablespoon garlic powder
1 tablespoon red pepper
1-1/4 cup whole wheat flour
1 tablespoon seasoning salt or
     creole seasoning
1 teaspoon cornstarch
2 tablespoons sriracha
4 cups vegetable oil

DIRECTIONS

In large bowl, mix eggs, garlic powder and red pepper. Place in a sealable container or large sealable bag. Cut wings into flats and drums. Add chicken to mixture and shake well. Marinate at least 2 -3 hours or overnight. Heat vegetable oil in deep pot or electric fryer. Add flour, sriracha, cornstarch and seasoning salt to sealable bag. Add 4-5 chicken wings and shake well. Repeat process until all wings have been fully coated. Let wings sit 2-3 minutes to helps coating adhere. Place chicken into hot oil (do not crowd the fryer—fry in smaller batches as needed), and cook 8–10 minutes, depending on the thickness/size of the wings. Drain on the rack. Repeat process until all wings have been cooked.

Notes

Spicy Stuffed Mushrooms

1 lb. spicy pan sausage
12 oz. whipped cream cheese
1 lb. whole mushrooms

DIRECTIONS

Crumble and pan fry sausage, making sure it is cooked thoroughly. Drain the meat on paper towels. In large bowl, combine meat and cream cheese, mixing well. Place mixture in the refrigerator for 1 hour. Preheat the oven to 375°F. Separate the caps from the mushroom stems. Lightly spray cookie sheet with oil. Fill mushroom caps with mixture and place on cookie sheet. Bake for 10-12 minutes.

Avocado Toast

1 large ripe avocado
2 tablespoons basil
1 clove garlic (minced)
Feta cheese
6-8 cherry tomatoes
1/4 teaspoon red pepper flakes (optional)
Pinch kosher salt
1 tablespoon balsamic vinegar
2 slices whole grain bread (or your choice of bread)

DIRECTIONS

Core and lightly mash avocado with fork, leaving lumps. Add basil and minced garlic, stir lightly. Toast bread in toaster or oven. Top toast with mixture adding Feta cheese and tomatoes. Drizzle with balsamic vinegar and salt to taste.

Notes

Spiced Lemon Watermelon

1 medium watermelon (cubed)
Juice of 1 large lemon
Mango Habanero seasoning

DIRECTIONS

Place watermelon cubes into a sealable bowl/container. Add lemon juice and toss to marinate the watermelon. Add seasoning to taste. Refrigerate for at least 1 hour before serving.

Smoked Salmon-Avocado Salad

1 (15 oz.) package arugula, thoroughly washed
6 radishes, thinly sliced
*2 (4 oz.) packages thinly sliced smoked salmon
1 avocado (sliced)

DIRECTIONS

Gently toss all ingredients together in large shallow bowl or platter. Serve with Lemon-Dijon Vinaigrette Dressing.

*Grilled salmon may be substituted for smoked salmon

Notes

Spinach and Fennel Salad with Chicken Breast and Red Wine Vinaigrette

Vinaigrette:

- 1/4 cup olive oil
- 2 tablespoons Red Wine Vinaigrette
- 1 clove garlic (minced)
- 2 shallots (minced)
- 1/4 teaspoon salt
- 1/4 teaspoon black pepper

DIRECTIONS

Whisk all ingredients together and allow to stand for 10 minutes to blend flavors.

Salad:

- 1 lb. precooked chicken breast strips, precooked
- (1) 6 oz. bag baby spinach
- 2 fennel bulbs (cut julienne)
- 2 cups red grapes (cut in half)
- 1/4 cup fresh mint (chopped)

DIRECTIONS

In a large bowl, toss all ingredients except chicken. Pour in vinaigrette and toss well to coat. Heat chicken according to directions and top desired amount on salad. Serve immediately.

Notes

Asian Inspired Shrimp and Scallop Sliders with Ginger Soy Dipping Sauce

5 tablespoons cooking oil
1/2 lb. shrimp (peeled and deveined)
3/4 lb. fresh sea scallops
2 cups shitake mushrooms (stemmed and sliced)
2 tablespoons fresh cilantro (chopped)
2 tablespoons chopped green onions (both white and green parts)
1 tablespoon mayonnaise
1 tablespoon honey Dijon mustard
1/3 cup soy sauce
3 tablespoons rice wine
1 tablespoon sugar
2 teaspoons fresh lime juice
1-1/2 teaspoons ginger juice
Sea salt
Black pepper
Slider buns

DIRECTIONS

Preheat the oven to 350°F. Heat 2 tablespoons oil in large non-stick skillet over medium high heat. Add mushrooms and sauté. Transfer to cutting board and chop. Coarsely chop shrimp and transfer to large bowl. Put scallops in food processor and pulse until smooth. Add scallops to shrimp, and combine with mushrooms, cilantro, green onions, mayonnaise, and mustard. Cover and chill for 30 minutes. With hands, form into patties about 2 inches in diameter and 1/2 inch thick, and place on baking sheet. Bake until lightly brown, then turn over and continue cooking until browned on both sides. Lightly brown slider buns on skillet. Construct slider with favorite toppings. Dip into dipping sauce as you eat.

Dipping Sauce:

Mix ginger juice, lime juice, rice wine, soy sauce, and sugar. Warm over medium heat stirring until the sugar dissolves. Transfer to small bowl for serving.

Notes

Hummus and Veggies

- 1 cup (store bought) hummus dip
- 1 avocado (sliced)
- 1 cup arugula or spinach
- 1/2 English cucumber (sliced)
- 1 cup baby carrots
- 6-8 cherry tomatoes (sliced in half)
- 4-6 asparagus stalks
  (sliced into sections
  approximately 2-inches in
  length)
- 1 tablespoon olive oil
- 2 slices pita bread

DIRECTIONS

Place hummus in small bowl on platter. Drizzle with olive oil. Arrange remaining ingredients on platter and serve.

Notes

Chicken Apple Pecan Salad

4 cups of cold water
3-1/2 teaspoons kosher salt
1 lb. (2) chicken breasts (boneless
    and skinless)
2 eggs (boiled and diced)
1/2 red onion (chopped)
1/2 green apple (diced)
2 tablespoons sweet pickle relish
1/2 cup sour cream
1/4 cup pecans (chopped)
Salt and pepper to taste
Baby corn (optional)
Pickled okra (optional)

DIRECTIONS

Fill a saucepan with 4 cups of cold water and chicken breasts in a saucepan. Be sure the water is cold because it allows the chicken to cook more gradually than it would if you just dumped them into already-boiling water. Season the water with the kosher salt. Turn the heat to medium and bring the water to a gentle boil. As soon as you see the surface of the water start to roll, flip the breasts over with tongs, remove the pot from heat, and cover it with a tightly-fitting lid. The chicken breasts will continue to cook gently in the hot water about 5-10 minutes, depending on how large or small the chicken breasts are. Remove chicken breasts from the water and let them rest on a cutting board for at least five minutes. Chop chicken to desired size and place in large bowl. Mix together eggs, onions, apples, relish, and sour cream. Add pecans and stir. Add salt and pepper to taste. Refrigerate until ready to serve. Serve on lettuce of choice as a salad or toasted bread for sandwich and garnish with baby corn and pickled okra.

Notes

Hold-the-Mayo Tuna Salad

1 family size (11 oz.) pouch tuna
    packed in water
2 celery stalks (chopped)
1/4 cup red onion (chopped)
1/4 cup red bell pepper
2 tablespoons olive oil
1 tablespoon capers
2 tablespoon kalamata olives (chopped)
2 tablespoon Castelvetrano olives (chopped)
1/8 cup carrots (shredded)
1 tablespoon lemon juice
1 tablespoon capers
1 tablespoon Dijon mustard
Coarse ground black pepper to taste
Tomato slices
1 avocado (mashed)
Romaine lettuce leaves

DIRECTIONS

Mix all ingredients in medium bowl. Add more oil if consistency is too dry. Chill for 30 minutes before serving to allow flavors to combine. Serve on lettuce with sliced tomatoes and avocado mash or as a sandwich.

Notes

Lobster Rolls

1 tablespoon Lemon Herb seasoning
3 lbs. cooked lobster meat
Juice of 1/2 lemon
1/3 cup mayonnaise
7 tablespoons unsalted butter, melted, divided
1/4 cup celery leaves (roughly chopped)
1/4 cup scallions (chopped)
4 brioche buns

DIRECTIONS

In a small bowl whisk the mayonnaise, 4 tablespoons of melted butter, celery, scallions, lemon juice, and the Lemon Herb seasoning. Add the lobster meat to the bowl and toss to coat. Chill for 3-4 hours before serving. Heat a grill pan or skillet to medium heat. Brush the inside of the buns with the remaining melted butter. Toast until golden. Divide the lobster salad among the buns and serve.

Notes

Cod Tacos

1 lb. cod (cut into chunks)
1/2 cup cilantro (chopped)
1/4 cup red onion (chopped)
1/4 cup lime juice
1 tablespoon chili powder
1 tablespoon cumin
2 tablespoons oil
1 large avocado (cut into chunks)
1 package wheat or corn tortillas
1/2 package cole slaw mix
1 cup pre-made mango salsa

DIRECTIONS

Mix chili powder, cumin and lime juice together in bowl. Add cod, sprinkle with salt, and allow to sit for 15 minutes; stir and sit for another 15 minutes. Heat oil in skillet and sear cod, turning every 2 minutes until golden brown and completely done. Heat tortillas in covered microwave container for 1 minute. Fill shells with cod and top with slaw, avocado, cilantro, and mango salsa.

Notes

Marinated Steaks with Lemon Cilantro Sauce

- 3 tablespoons red wine vinegar
- 2 tablespoons brown mustard
- 1 tablespoon pecan oil
- (2) 6 oz. steaks

DIRECTIONS

Mix vinegar, mustard and oil, and pour over steaks. Marinate steaks overnight. Grill steaks approximately 5-6 minutes each side until desired doneness.

Lemon Cilantro Sauce

- 1 tablespoon cilantro
- 3 tablespoons pecan oil
- 1 tablespoon garlic
- 1 lemon
- Pinch kosher salt

DIRECTIONS

Cut lemon in half. Place on hot grill. Flat side down and grill until browned. Mix all remaining ingredients and squeeze the juice of grilled lemons into the mixture. Pour mixture over steaks and serve.

Notes

Spicy Boil

3 tablespoons Zatarain's crab boil
 (extra spicy or mild)
6 Andouille sausage links
 (sliced into 1/2inch pieces)
1 lb. red and/or yellow new potatoes
1 cup sliced carrots chips
10 mini corn on the cobs
 (cut in half)
2 lbs. shrimp (optional)
1 lemon (sliced)

DIRECTIONS

Bring 2 quarts of water to boil in a large pot. Add Zatarain's crab boil, lemon, sausage, corn, potatoes, and carrots. Boil 15-20 minutes. Add shrimp and boil 1 minute (optional). Remove from heat and let sit until lukewarm before serving.

Notes

Pesto Spicy Pasta

(1) 13 oz. bag/box short pasta
(penne, elbow macaroni,
bowties, etc.)
1 teaspoon olive oil
2 cloves garlic (chopped)
8 oz. of pesto (fresh or pre-made)
4-6 spicy Italian sausages
2 tablespoons of basil (chopped)
10-12 mushrooms to taste
(optional)
Olives – pitted (optional)
Dash of sea salt

DIRECTIONS

In a large pot, add 1 teaspoon of olive oil to water and a dash of salt. Bring to boil, and cook the pasta per the package directions. Drain pasta and return to pot. Add pesto to pasta and mix. Cover and set aside. In a skillet, fry sausage until done. Remove sausage from skillet. In drippings, add garlic and cook until it begins to turn tender. Add mushrooms and sauté until tender. In large bowl, combine sausage, pasta, garlic, mushrooms, basil, olives, and mushrooms to pasta. Mix well and cover. Allow flavors to blend for 15-20 minutes before serving.

Notes

Lime Marinated Mango

1 large ripe mango, sliced
1 lime, juiced
1 pinch of Tajin seasoning

DIRECTIONS

Place the mango slices in a large bowl.
Pour in lime juice and toss. Add Tajin seasoning to taste.

Chill for 30 minutes and serve.

Notes

Grilled Glazed Carrots

    5 large carrots (sliced)
    2 tablespoons brown spicy mustard
    1 teaspoon olive oil

DIRECTIONS

In a container, mix olive oil and brown spicy mustard. Add carrots and marinate for 2-3 hours. Grill for 6-8 minutes, turning once halfway through.

Italian Style Spinach

    (1) 8 oz. bag spinach, prewashed
    2 garlic cloves (minced)
    1/2 teaspoon crushed red pepper flakes
    2 teaspoons olive oil
    1 lemon
    Pinch sea salt

DIRECTIONS

Add garlic cloves and olive oil in pan and sauté for 1 minute. Pat dry spinach to rid excess water and add to pan with red pepper. Stir for 2-3 minutes until spinach is wilted. Drain and remove to serving bowl. Squeeze on lemon juice to taste and add pinch of sea salt.

Notes

Cilantro Rice

- 1 pouch instant rice
- 2 tablespoons fresh cilantro (chopped)
- 1 teaspoon garlic (pressed)
- 1 teaspoon onion powder
- 2 tablespoons salted butter
- 2 tablespoons fresh squeezed lime juice

DIRECTIONS

Cook rice according to directions. Rinse and drain. In medium bowl, combine all ingredients. Mix well and serve hot.

Sautéed Snap Peas

- 1/2 lb. fresh snap peas
- 1/4 yellow bell pepper
  (cut into strips)
- 1/4 orange bell pepper
  (cut into strips)
- 2 tablespoon extra-virgin olive oil
- 1 clove garlic (minced)

DIRECTIONS

In a sauté pan, add olive oil and minced garlic and sauté. Add peas, cover pan and toss. Add bell pepper, cover and toss again. Cook until tender, about 8 minutes.

Notes

Tempura Vegetables

*2 zucchini (cut into spears)
1 cup all-purpose flour
1 cup club soda or seltzer water
2 tablespoons Hellmann's mayonnaise
1 tablespoon cornstarch
2 cups vegetable oil
Pinch Sea salt
Dash pepper
*You may substitute squash, carrots, mushrooms,
    or cauliflower for zucchini if desired.

DIRECTIONS

Create tempura batter by slowly mixing flour, club soda (club soda must be extremely cold), mayonnaise, and cornstarch (leaving some lumps). Heat oil in deep skillet to 400°F. Pat dry vegetables and dip into tempura mix, coating well. Separately place vegetables into hot oil, do not overcrowd. Turn often to cook all sides until golden brown (7-8 minutes.) Drain on paper towel and dust with sea salt and pepper to taste.

Lemon & Rosemary Roasted Yukon Gold Potatoes

2 lbs. Yukon Gold potatoes (quartered)
1 stick (1/2 cup) butter
2 tablespoons fresh rosemary
1/4 cup fresh squeezed lemon juice
Sea salt
Cracked black pepper

DIRECTIONS

Preheat the oven to 375°F. Melt butter in roasting pan; add potatoes and rosemary, mixing well. Place in oven and cover. Cook for about 20-25 minutes until potatoes are tender. Remove from oven and pour lemon juice over potatoes, sprinkle with salt and pepper to taste.

Roasted Veggies and Brown Rice

1 lb. zucchini (sliced)
1 lb. yellow squash (sliced)
3 large carrots (thinly sliced)
1 large sweet onion
1 large red bell pepper (diced)
3 tablespoons olive oil
1 tablespoon seasoned salt
1/2 teaspoon white pepper
2 cups cooked brown rice

DIRECTIONS

Preheat the oven to 450°F. Toss together all ingredients except brown rice, until well coated. Place vegetables in shallow pan. Bake for about 20-30 minutes until slightly crisp. Serve atop brown rice.

Pan Fried Cabbage

1 lb. peppered bacon
1 large head cabbage (chopped)
1 large onion (sliced)
1 medium red bell pepper (sliced)
1 medium green bell pepper (sliced)
Salt
White pepper

DIRECTIONS

Place bacon in a large skillet and cook over medium-high heat, turning occasionally, until evenly browned, about 10 minutes. Drain the bacon slices on paper towels; crumble when cooled. Drain all but 3 tablespoons of bacon drippings from skillet. Cook and stir cabbage, onion, red bell peppers, and green bell peppers in the remaining bacon drippings until tender and lightly browned, about 20 minutes. Fold bacon into cabbage mixture. Season with salt and white pepper to taste.

Notes

Cajun Cooked Kale

*2 bunches fresh kale (chopped)
1 /2 lb. smoked turkey necks
1 large onion (chopped)
1 red bell pepper (chopped)
4 cups chicken broth
4 large garlic cloves (sliced)
1 tablespoon Cajun seasoning
*Mustard, collard or turnip greens may be substituted if desired.

DIRECTIONS

In Dutch oven, bring to boil chicken broth, add turkey necks, onion, peppers, and garlic. Reduce heat and simmer for about 10 minutes with lid on pot. Add kale and Cajun seasoning, cook until tender about 30 minutes.

Savory Roasted Butternut Squash

(1) 10 oz. bag frozen butternut squash
2 tablespoons olive oil
2 garlic cloves (minced)
1 teaspoon dried rosemary
Sea salt
Black pepper

DIRECTIONS

Preheat the oven to 400°F. Toss butternut squash with olive oil, rosemary, and garlic in a large bowl. Season with salt and black pepper. Arrange coated squash on a baking sheet. Roast in the preheated oven until squash is tender and lightly browned, 25 to 30 minutes.

Notes

Lemony English Peas

(1) 8 oz. bag frozen English peas
2 tablespoons butter
1/4 cup heavy cream
1/2 teaspoon flour
1 large shallot (finely chopped)
2 teaspoons fresh chives
1/4 lemon zest

DIRECTIONS

Parboil peas by adding them to boiling salted water and quickly remove. Drain peas and shock with ice to stop cooking. In medium saucepan, melt butter over low heat. Add shallots and sauté until soft, about 2-3 minutes. Add the heavy cream, chives and lemon zest and bring to boil. Add peas and flour, reduce heat and simmer. Cook until the cream has thickened clinging peas and peas are tender and hot.

Notes

Stuffed Tomatoes

4 large tomatoes
1 tablespoon butter
1 cup yellow onion (chopped)
1 cup fresh spinach (rough chopped)
1/4 cup basil (chopped)
1/4 cup prepared pesto
1 oz. shaved Parmesan cheese
I pouch microwavable brown rice
Salt
Pepper

DIRECTIONS

Preheat the oven to 350°F. Cut off tops of tomatoes, about 1/4-1/2 inch, and discard. Cust a small slice from the bottom so that they will stand flat. Carefully scoop out pulp, leaving the shell intact. Sprinkle shells lightly with salt and strain and save juice from the pulp. Discard pulp. Melt butter in skillet and caramelize the onion. Add spinach and cook for about 3 minutes until spinach is wilted. Add tomato juice and rice. Cook until warmed throughout. Remove from heat, add basil and about 1/4 teaspoon salt and pepper to taste. Place tomato shells on baking dish and fill. Bake in oven about 15 minutes. Top with cheese and pesto.

Stuffed Sweet Potatoes

1/2 cup arugula
1 large sweet potato
2 tablespoons bleu or goat cheese
Pinch cayenne pepper
1/8 teaspoon cumin
Pinch salt

DIRECTIONS

Preheat the oven to 350°F. Bake sweet potato in oven for about 30 minutes. Place sweet potato on plate and cut lengthwise. Mix spices together and sprinkle onto the potato. Add goat cheese and top with arugula.

Sweet Potato Fries

2-3 red sweet potatoes
(cut into wedges with skin on)
2 tablespoons olive oil
Cajun seasoning

DIRECTIONS

Preheat the oven to 350°F. In large bowl, pour in oil and seasoning. Add sweet potatoes, stirring to thoroughly coat with oil and seasoning. Place potato wedges in single layer on large flat cookie sheet and bake until tender, about 20 minutes.

Fried Green Tomatoes

1 large egg (lightly beaten)
1/2 cup buttermilk
1/2 cup fish fry seasoning
1/2 cup panko bread crumbs
1/4 cup all purpose flour
2 lbs. medium size firm green tomatoes
(sliced into 1/3 inches thick slices)
1 cup vegetable oil
1 tablespoon salt

DIRECTIONS

Heat oil in deep fryer to 350°F. Lightly sprinkle salt on sliced tomatoes to release water. This will allow the flour to adhere to the tomatoes. Place flour, panko, and fish fry seasoning into separate shallow dishes. Beat egg and buttermilk in a separate bowl. Dredge tomatoes through the flour, then the egg mixture, then the fish fry mix, and lastly, the breadcrumbs. If breadcrumbs do not stick, dredge tomatoes once again through the egg mixture and then through the crumbs. Add only a few slices at a time to fryer so they may be able to cook evenly, about 2-3 minutes. Drain on paper towel and serve.

Grilled Globe Eggplant

1 eggplant (sliced about 1/4 inch thick)
3 tablespoons olive oil
1/4 cup fresh oregano (finely chopped)
1/4 cup fresh thyme (finely chopped)
1/4 cup fresh basil (finely chopped)
2 cloves garlic (minced)
1 tablespoon balsamic vinegar

DIRECTIONS

Lightly salt eggplant and allow to rest for a few minutes. Now combine the oil, vinegar, garlic, herbs, salt, and pepper. Let it sit to absorb the flavors for about 15 minutes. Brush eggplant with oil and herb mixture all over, ensuring that the herbs get distributed well. Place on a lightly greased grill and grill for about 15-20 minutes, until tender, flipping halfway through.

Oven Roasted Herb Potatoes

1 lb. new potatoes, red or yellow
1 tablespoon olive oil
1 teaspoon Tuscan Heat seasoning
1 teaspoon Italian Seasoning or oregano
1 Teaspoon Tony Chachere's Original Seasoning

DIRECTIONS

Preheat the oven to 375°F. Cut potatoes into fours or slices as even as possible to ensure even cooking. Add olive oil and potatoes to a 9x9-inch glass or nonstick pan. Mix well to coat potatoes. Add seasonings and continue to mix with hands to evenly coat. Cook for 15 minutes and flip potatoes over. Cook another 15 minutes until tender.

Notes

Fried Plantains

2-3 plantains
Sea Salt or seasoning salt
Vegetable/Canola oil

DIRECTIONS

Heat oil in fryer or deep fryer to 400°F.
Cut plantains into 1/4-thick slices.
Drop into hot oil. Cook 3-4 minutes.
Add pinch of salt or seasoning salt to taste.

Grilled Asparagus

1 bunch of asparagus
2 tablespoons olive oil
Dash sea salt
Dash pepper

DIRECTIONS

Coat cookie sheet with olive oil and roll asparagus in oil until well coated. Sprinkle asparagus with sea salt and pepper. Cook on grill until tender (about 5-7 minutes depending upon thickness.)

Notes

Vegetable Kabobs

Mushrooms
Cherry tomatoes
1 red onion
1 yellow squash (sliced into
1/4-inch thick coins)
1 zucchini (sliced into 1/4-inch
thick coins)
1 orange bell pepper
1 red bell pepper
2 tablespoons olive oil
Tajin seasoning

DIRECTIONS

Reserve sliced zucchini and squash. Cut onions and bell peppers into even pieces. Place all cut vegetables on cookie sheet and coat with olive oil. Add vegetables to skewers mixing colors, and sprinkle with a dash of Tajin. Cook on open grill for 2-3 minutes each side turning often, making sure not to let flame touch.

Oven Roasted Eggplant

1 globe eggplant (sliced into
1/4 to 1/2 inch thick circles)
1 tablespoon salt
2 tablespoons salt-free
Mediterranean seasoning
1 tablespoon olive oil

DIRECTIONS

Preheat the oven to 400°F. Place eggplant slices on platter and drizzle with salt and allow to rest for 10 minutes. Rinse and pat dry. Lightly coat bottom of pan with oil and arrange eggplant slices. Sprinkle with Mediterranean seasoning, turn over, and sprinkle other side with Mediterranean seasoning. Place in oven and bake for about 10 minutes, turn over and bake for about 10 minutes. Sprinkle with a dash of salt to taste and serve.

Grilled Cauliflower Steaks

2 large cauliflower heads
2 tablespoons olive oil
Kosher salt
Black Pepper
1 tablespoon Butter (melted)
Lemon wedges

DIRECTIONS

Heat the grill. Create a cauliflower steak by cutting a thick slice (1/4 inches) of raw cauliflower from the center of a cauliflower head, leaving the stem intact. You can get two thick slices (steaks) from one large head of cauliflower. Brush with olive oil. Place on hot grill. Grill for about 1 minute and turn. You'll know when cauliflower is cooked when a sharp knife pierces easily into the flesh. Take care not to overcook cauliflower as it can turn mushy. Remove from grill once done. Brush with butter, sprinkle with salt and pepper to taste. Serve with lemon wedges.

Notes

BREAKFAST
AND BRUNCH

Quick Quiche Cups

1 package tortillas
    (flour, wheat, or corn)
3 eggs (slightly beaten)
1-1/2 cups whole milk
6 tablespoons green onion (chopped)
1/2 to 1/3 cup diced ham or
    crumbled breakfast sausage
    (cooked)
1 cup white Cheddar cheese (shredded)
Salt and pepper to taste
Picante sauce or sriracha

DIRECTIONS

Preheat the oven to 375°F. Press individual tortillas into muffin pan that has been lightly sprayed. Trim off excess tortilla and set aside. Tortilla should completely cover the inside of each individual muffin section of the pan. Mix all ingredients, except cheese, together in large mixing bowl, adding salt and pepper to taste. Pour egg mixture into the individual muffin sections, sprinkle top with cheese. Bake for about 20 minutes. Let stand about 10 minutes before serving. Top with picante sauce or sriracha if you like.

Notes

Best Bacon

12 slices thick cut bacon
1/4 cup candied jalapeño slices
1/4 cup maple syrup

DIRECTIONS

Preheat the oven to 375°F. In bowl, mix jalapeños and syrup. Arrange bacon strips in oven-safe shallow pan. Pour jalapeños and syrup over the bacon, turn over bacon to evenly coat. Let stand for 30 minutes. Pour off any excess syrup. Bake in oven until bacon is crisp. Remove bacon and allow to drain on paper towels.

Cranberry and Pistachio Pancakes

Buttermilk pancake mix
1/3 cup pistachio (chopped)
1/3 cup cranberries
Butter
Maple syrup

DIRECTIONS

Follow directions to make 12 pancakes, adding the pistachio and cranberries to the mix. Stir until moistened. Heat griddle on medium heat with 1 tablespoon butter. For each pancake, pour about 1/4 cup batter, cooking for about 1-2 minutes (until bubbles form on top) before flipping. Add butter to the griddle as you flip pancakes to keep from sticking and to encourage nice browning. Serve warm with heated syrup. Top with additional cranberries and pistachios if desired.

Notes

B&B Stuffed Bell Peppers

4 large red bell peppers (cut lengthwise
    in half and all pulp and seeds removed)
1/2 lb. ground pork breakfast sausage
1 cup sweet onion (chopped)
1 1/2 cups chicken broth
1 cup heavy cream
1/4 cup flat leaf parsley (chopped)
3-4 oz. shredded sharp Cheddar cheese
1/2 cup instant grits

DIRECTIONS

Preheat the oven to 350°F. Place red bell pepper shells on baking sheet. Crumble and brown sausage in skillet, adding onion about halfway through the cooking process. Bring chicken broth to boil in medium saucepan, add grits, reduce heat, stirring occasionally. Pour heavy cream, cooked sausage mix, and cheese into the grits. Stir well. Allow to sit for about 10 minutes to absorb all liquid. Spoon into red bell pepper shells. Bake about 30 minutes. Top with parsley and salt and pepper to taste.

Sunshine Toast

4 slices frozen Texas toast
4 eggs
1/4 cup tomatoes (chopped)
2 tablespoons parsley or cilantro (chopped)
2 tablespoons chives (chopped)
2 tablespoons Monterey jack cheese
8 slices bacon (cooked crispy)

DIRECTIONS

Use a cookie cutter to cut out center of each slice of toast. Heat non-stick pan, placing 1-2 slices of toast in the pan. Crack one egg and pour into the hole in the toast. Cover pan and allow the egg to cook. Use spatula to remove from pan. Place on plate for serving. Toss tomatoes, parsley/cilantro. Chives and cheese together in bowl and use as a topping on the eggs. Serve with 2 slices of bacon or crumble bacon on top.

Notes

No-cook Fruit & Yogurt Squares

2-3 cups original Grape Nuts cereal
3 cups vanilla-flavored Greek yogurt
2 cups frozen or fresh mixed berries
    (strawberries, raspberries, blueberries, and blackberries)
1/2 cup walnuts
1/2 cup granola
Honey
Mint

DIRECTIONS

Fill the bottom of 8x8-inch pan with cereal, pressing down and compacting about 1-inch to 1-1/2 inches thick. Stir the yogurt, making sure all liquid is mixed with the yogurt and make a layer atop the oats. Place mixed fruit atop the yogurt and sprinkle with granola and nuts. Cover with plastic wrap and refrigerate overnight. Cut into squares and gently remove with spatula. Drizzle with honey and top with a sprig of mint.

Notes

PB&B Overnight Oatmeal

(1) 6 oz. carton plain yogurt
2/3 cup regular rolled oats (uncooked)
2/3 cup milk
1/4 cup banana (sliced)
2 tablespoons honey
1 tablespoon chia seeds or flax seeds
1 tablespoon peanut butter
2 pint-size Mason jars with lids

DIRECTIONS

In a medium bowl, combine yogurt, oats, milk, half of the banana slices, honey, chia seeds (or flax seeds) and peanut butter. Transfer to pint size mason jar and cover with lid overnight. Serve in the jar with slices of banana on top.

Notes

Ham and Asparagus Strata

1 loaf Italian or French rustic bread,
    cut into 1 1/2-inch cubes,
    about 5 cups total of bread cubes
8 oz. asparagus spears (woody stems removed,
    cut into 2-inch-long lengths)
Salt (for blanching water)
1 medium bowl of ice water
2 tablespoons softened butter (for buttering the dish)
8 oz. ham, cut into 1/4-inch cubes, about 2 cups
1/4 cup sweet onion (chopped)
1/4 cup green onion (chopped)
8 oz. Gruyere cheese, grated, about 1 cup, packed
6 eggs
1 1/4 cups cream
1-1/2 cups milk
1 teaspoon salt
1 teaspoon dried tarragon (or thyme)
1/4 teaspoon ground black pepper
Salt
Olive oil

DIRECTIONS

Cook asparagus in boiling salted water for about 5 minutes. Drain and set aside. Grease 3-quart casserole dish with butter. Spread half of the bread into the bottom of dish, top with cheese, onion, and chives. Top with half of the asparagus and half of the ham. In a bowl, whisk together the eggs, milk, and cream, pour over the mixture, and top off with another layer of remaining bread, asparagus, and ham. Sprinkle tarragon on top. Cover and refrigerate 8-24 hours. Preheat the oven to 375˚F. Bake uncovered for 45-50 minutes. Let stand for 15 minutes before serving. Add salt and pepper to taste. Drizzle with olive oil.

Notes

Blueberry Pancakes with Ricotta

1/2 cup all-purpose flour
2 teaspoons baking powder
1/2 teaspoon salt
1 cup ricotta cheese
4 egg yolks
3 tablespoons sugar
1/4 cup milk
1-1/2 cups fresh or frozen blueberries
4 egg whites
Blueberry Lemon Syrup

DIRECTIONS

In large bowl, combine flour, baking powder and salt. In medium bowl, whisk together cheese, egg yolks, and sugar. Add cheese mixture to the flour mixture, stirring until smooth. Add milk, then fold in the blueberries. In small bowl, mix egg whites with electric mixer until stiff peaks form. Gently fold beaten egg into the batter. Do not over beat. For each pancake, pour about 1/4 cup batter onto heated griddle. Cook on each side until golden brown, about 1-2 minutes per side. Serve with Blueberry Lemon Syrup or your favorite syrup.

Blueberry Lemon Syrup

1 cup sugar
1 cup water
1/3 cup lemon juice
1 teaspoon grated lemon zest
2 packages (6 oz. or 1 1/4 cups each) blueberries

DIRECTIONS

Combine all ingredients in saucepan and bring to boil over medium-high heat. Reduce to medium low heat and simmer 20 minutes. Strain and allow to cool.

Mini Egg and Salami Skillets

4 eggs
3 tablespoons milk
1 tablespoon flour
1 tablespoon chives
*4 slices peppered salami
Cheese
Salt and pepper
2 tomato slices
*Prosciutto ham may be substituted if desired.

DIRECTIONS

Heat the oven to 350°F. Place 2 slices of salami into bottom of individual serving size small skillet or oven-proof ramekins. Mix all other ingredients except tomato slices in medium bowl and pour even amount into each skillet, placing one tomato slice atop each. Return to oven and bake until center is done, about 10 minutes. Serve immediately.

Notes

INDEX

DISCLAIMER

Neither Bea nor Vernita claims to be a professional chef, cook, or nutritionist. The recipes shared in this book are created according to their own personal preferences. These recipes do contain nuts, seafood, dairy and gluten products. Please be mindful when reviewing the recipes and make substitutions that are best suited to your own personal preferences and health concerns

www.pinch-dash-done.com

THANK YOU

We are extremely grateful to everyone that worked with us to help make this project come to fruition. This cookbook holds countless hours of work coupled with your help—including taste-testing in our labs, offering suggestions, updating old recipes with a new twist, giving professional guidance, and most of all, gracing us with your prayers for success. We are blessed to have a village that is so supportive and encouraging.

We sincerely thank you all.

This book is just the first in a series and we look forward to working with you on our future projects coming down the pipeline.

Please join us on our website for more information @ www.pinch-dash-done.com

To be continued.......

CPSIA information can be obtained
at www.ICGtesting.com
Printed in the USA
LVHW011017291220
675237LV00018B/3239

9 781735 546315